52 Week Devotional for Boys
Ages 6-9

HENDRICKSON
PUBLISHERS

ROSE
KiDZ

www.hendricksonrose.com

52 Week Devotional for Boys
Ages 6-9

Diane Cory
H. Michael Brewer and
Janet Neff Brewer

Gotta Have God 52 Week Devotional for Boys Ages 6-9
Copyright 2016 by Rose Publishing, LLC
Compiled from Gotta Have God for Boys Ages 6-9 series, Vols. 1-3 (various copyrights)

Rose Kidz® is an imprint of
Rose Publishing, LLC
P.O. Box 3473
Peabody, Massachusetts 01961-3473 USA
www.hendricksonrose.com
All rights reserved.

Cover and interior design by Nancy L. Haskins
Illustrations by Aline L. Heiser and Dave Carleson

ISBN: 978-1-58411-175-7
RoseKidz® reorder# L46971
JUVENILE NONFICTION/Religion/Devotion & Prayer

Printed in the United States
Printed September 2018

Contents

Just for YOU!

Hey, guys, Gotta Have God is a special book just for you. This book will help you learn more about your heavenly Father. There are 52 weeks of devotionals and activities—that's a whole year's worth. Each week you will have two devotions to read plus five activities to help you get closer to God.

We encourage you to do one page every day. To help you memorize the week's Bible verse, practice saying it out loud each day. At the end of the week, say the verse without any mistakes. You can do it!

Each day you'll have a special time with God. Take time to talk to Him through prayer as you go through this book. Start today and learn why *you gotta have God!*

God's Awesome Word

Every word of God is flawless.
– Proverbs 30:5

The Bible Is True

A lie is when someone says something that isn't true. Books that are called *fiction* tell interesting, just-for-fun stories that aren't true. They may tell part of the truth, but they don't tell all the truth. *Nonfiction* books tell the facts.

There is one book that *always* tells us the truth. This book is the best book of all. It's called the Bible. The word "Bible" means "the Book." The Bible is God's special letter written for all people—including you. God used people to write down his words for us to read.

The Bible tells us about God and everything he made. From reading the Bible, we know that God made land, sky, stars, sun, moon, water, plants, animals, and people. The Bible also tells us about God's power and how much he loves people. God tells us in his Word—the Bible—that he made each one of us. Everything in the Bible is true because it comes from God!

Your Turn

1. Can you name some things the Bible says God made?

2. When will you read your Bible each day?

_____

_____

_____

Prayer

Thank you, God, for the Bible—your message to me. Help me remember to read the Bible every day. Amen.

God's Awesome Word

Every word of God is flawless.
– Proverbs 30:5

Something Is Wrong

Some things aren't true, but the Bible always is. It's always good to read. Other books might not be. Look at the books. Circle the one that will help you live the best way. Cross out the books that might be bad for you. Draw a square around those you might want to read but should ask your parents first.

Prayer

Dear God, thank you for the Bible. I know that all the information in the Bible is true and from you. Help me read books that are pleasing to you. Amen.

God's Awesome Word

Every word of God is flawless.
– Proverbs 30:5

The Bible Is True

Can you use the code to solve the puzzle and find an important fact about Jesus?

A B C D E F G H I J K L M N
1 2 3 4 5 6 7 8 9 10 11 12 13 14

O P Q R S T U V W X Y Z
15 16 17 18 19 20 21 22 23 24 25 26

ANYONE WHO HAS
1 14 25 15 14 5   23 8 15   8 1 19

SEEN ME   HAS
19 5 5 14 13 5   8 1 19

SEEN   THE
19 5 5 14   20 8 5

FATHER   JOHN
6 1 20 8 5 18   10 15 8 14   14:9

Prayer

Dear God, help me read my Bible each day so I will know what you are like. Amen.

God's Awesome Word

Every word of God is flawless.

– Proverbs 30:5

God wants to Talk to You

Mom whispered in Josh's ear, "You're a great kid."

Josh whispered back in her ear, "You're a great mom."

Have you realized that someone in your family talks to you every day? Grandparents and friends talk to you on the phone or by texting. Maybe you talk to the mail person or the crossing guard at school. God wants to talk to you each day. His Word, the Bible, is one way he shares his wisdom. God gave the Bible so you can know how much he cares for his creation. He wants you to read the Bible so he can tell you about everything he does. He wants you to find out how much he loves you.

God wants to talk to you. He wants to help you get the most out of life. The Word of God was written many years ago, but what it says is still true and great for you to know.

There's a great truth in the Bible that is really exciting. God sent his Son, Jesus, to tell people about him. Jesus was like a walking book. He told people about God.

Your Turn

1. God talks to you when you read the Bible. How do you talk to Him?
2. The Word of God is active. What do you think that means?

_____

_____

_____

_____

Prayer

God, I want to know you and hear from you. I believe your Word—everything in the Bible—is true. I will listen to you. Thank you for sending Jesus to help me. Amen.

God's Awesome Word

Every word of God is flawless.
– Proverbs 30:5

The Peanut Butter Jar

Have you had a peanut butter sandwich? The peanut butter sticks to the roof of your mouth, doesn't it? Look at the jar of peanut butter. Fill it with words from the Bible that stick in your mind. You can write your favorite Bible verses in the jar too.

Prayer

Dear God, I pray that your truths in the Bible will stick in my heart. I want to know you more. Amen.

God's Awesome Word

Every word of God is flawless.
– Proverbs 30:5

Texting God

The Bible is like a letter God has written to you. Pretend you are texting God. Tell him about you and how much you want to know him better.

Prayer

Dear God, I want to talk to you. I know that when I talk to you, you hear me. Thank you for listening. Amen.

God's Awesome Word

Every word of God is flawless.
– Proverbs 30:5

My Promise to God

Promise God that you will do your best to read your Bible and pray every day. Fill in the blanks of this note to God. Copy it and put it where you will see it every day.

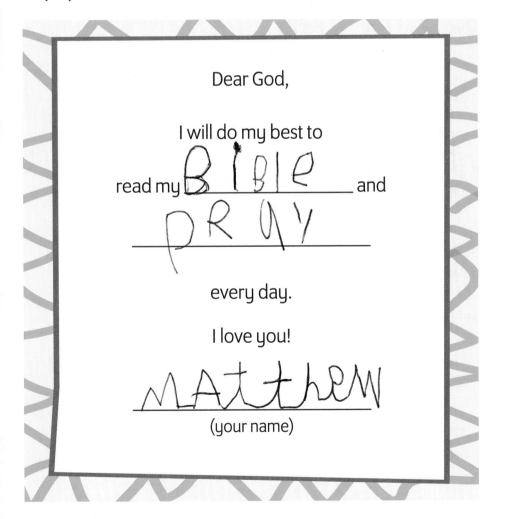

Dear God,

I will do my best to

read my B I B l e and

P R A Y

every day.

I love you!

MATthew

(your name)

Prayer

God, I know that if I read my Bible and pray to you, I will know you better and be happier. Help me remember to do these things every day. Amen.

God Created the Heavens and Earth

It is I who made the earth and created mankind on it.
– Isaiah 45:12

God's Awesome Creation

Saw, hammer, tape measure...what tools go into a tool belt? You can build things with a hammer, saw, nails, and wood. Imagine creating a tree house without using any tools or material!

What tools did God use to create the world? He didn't use any! God only needed to use his powerful voice. He spoke the words and the heavens and earth appeared in space.

Some of the first words in the Bible are "God created the heavens and the earth." These words tell us God is a creator. His tool belt is full of power to create what he wants.

Your Turn

1. Why do you think God created the earth?
2. What can you make with the tools you have?

_____

_____

_____

_____

_____

_____

Prayer

Thank you, God, for creating the world. Thank you for loving me enough to provide a place for me to live. Amen.

God Created the Heavens and Earth

It is I who made the earth and created mankind on it.
– Isaiah 45:12

Tree House Creation

God made plants for you to enjoy. Draw your own tree house in the tree.

Prayer

Thank You, God, for the many wonderful plants and animals you created.
Amen.

God Created the Heavens and Earth

It is I who made the earth and created mankind on it.

– Isaiah 45:12

A Flashlight at Night

God made the moon and the stars. They help us to see at night. Doesn't it look like God is shining a flashlight on the Earth? Can you draw stars and a moon below the flashlight?

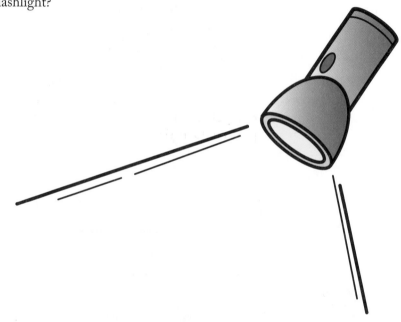

Prayer

God, I see your work in the day and night sky. Thank you for being my powerful and creative God. Amen.

God Created the Heavens and Earth

It is I who made the earth and created mankind on it.
– Isaiah 45:12

Things that Grow

Are you a tree climber? Have you ever played a spy game in the bushes? Without a tree, there would be nothing to climb. Without bushes, there would be no place to hide. Did you know God created all the trees and all the bushes? He spoke and the trees appeared. God spoke again and the bushes appeared. He spoke again and flowers and grass grew.

God wants you to enjoy climbing trees and playing spy games. He wants you to eat fruit and vegetables. God created everything, and he can create anything at any time. He created the plants and animals for you to enjoy. You can read about how God made plants in Genesis 1:11-13 in your Bible.

Your Turn

1. Can you name some plants and animals God created?
   How many can you name in one minute?
2. What kinds of fruit and vegetables do you like to eat?

_____

_____

_____

_____

Prayer

God, I enjoy playing outside where I can see the plants and animals You created. Thank you for all your creation. Amen.

God Created the Heavens and Earth

It is I who made the earth and created mankind on it.
– Isaiah 45:12

God Created Everything

If God can make the earth, what else can he do? Write on the tool belt some of the things God can do.

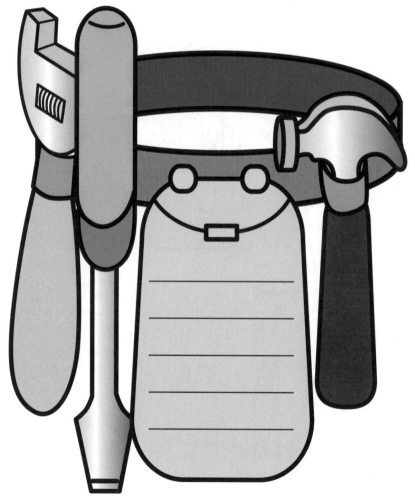

Prayer

Dear God, you can do everything! I am so glad you are always here with me. Amen.

God Created the Heavens and Earth

It is I who made the earth and created mankind on it.

– Isaiah 45:12

God's Farm

God made all the animals on the earth. What is your favorite animal? Draw a picture of it. What does your animal eat? Draw that too.

Prayer

God, I am so glad you made the animals. You made many different kinds, and they are good for many things. Thank you. Amen.

God Created the Heavens and Earth

It is I who made the earth and created mankind on it.

– Isaiah 45:12

God Created You

God made you just the way you are! Draw what you look like and then write what you would tell God about the way he made you.

Prayer

Dear God, thank you for all the love and care you showed when you created me. Help me be thankful every day for my life. Amen.

God Is Easy to Find

*You will seek me and find me
when you seek me with all your heart.*
– Jeremiah 29:13

Finding God

"It couldn't have just walked away!"

"I know I put it right here!"

"I'm not going to stop looking until I find it."

You can't always find things you look for, but God isn't a thing, he is a real being. Can you talk with your pen or ball? Can you call your pen or ball? Seeking God is not like looking for a missing pen or a football. When you look for God, you will always find him.

A lost ball may not be found for months. You will never lose God. God promised to be with you when you look for him. The book of Jeremiah in the Bible says that when you call out to God with your heart, he will hear you and be with you.

Your Turn

1. Is God real? How do you know he is real?
2. How can you find God?
3. How can you help your friends when they are looking for God?

_____

_____

_____

_____

_____

Prayer

Thank you, God, that I can call to you and you will always answer me.
I seek you with all my heart. Please show me you are here with me. Amen.

God Is Easy to Find

You will seek me and find me when you seek me with all your heart.
– Jeremiah 29:13

Police Lights and Fire Bells

God uses people like police and firefighters and your parents to help watch over you. On the police light and fire bell, write down the names of people God has helping him watch over you.

Prayer

Thank you, God, for police and firefighters. They work hard to keep me safe. And thank you for my parents because they watch over me too. Amen.

God Is Easy to Find

You will seek me and find me when you seek me with all your heart.

– Jeremiah 29:13

Track and Field Day

Do you worry? Do you get scared? In the middle of the racetrack, write down things you worry about. Psalm 23:1 says, "The LORD is my shepherd." You are one of his sheep, so he will protect you. Draw a line from each boy to the safety of the Shepherd.

Prayer

Dear God, sometimes I worry about things. But I know now that I can give you my worries and you will help me. Thank you! Amen.

God Is Easy to Find

You will seek me and find me
when you seek me with all your heart.
– Jeremiah 29:13

The Master Builder

Have you ever built anything? Building a model plane or birdhouse takes instructions or blueprints. What would you like to build?

Casey's dad was a furniture builder. He would often invite Casey to help in his workshop. Before they would start any project, they would first review the plan for the piece. Like Casey's dad, God shared his plans and invited his people to help him build special projects, like Noah and the Ark and Solomon and the Temple. God also has special plans for his people.

Your Turn

1. Read these Bible Verses and answer: What plans for Abraham did God have for him and his family? Genesis 12:2
2. What kinds of plans does God have for you? Jeremiah 29:11

_____

_____

_____

_____

Prayer

Dear God, I want you to be my expert builder and I will be your trainee. Teach me to use your tools to live life the right way. Amen.

God Is Easy to Find

You will seek me and find me when you seek me with all your heart.

– Jeremiah 29:13

Pesky Flies

Jesus is your Shepherd. Do you know what a shepherd does? He protects his sheep even from pesky flies. Do you ever want to do something that isn't good for you? Write down some things you know aren't good to do. Then ask God to help you stay safe.

Prayer

God, will you help me? I want you to be my Shepherd. Help me keep out of trouble and stay safe. Thank you. Amen.

God Is Easy to Find

You will seek me and find me when you seek me with all your heart.
– Jeremiah 29:13

Trading Cards

Do you have any baseball cards? Friends often like to trade sports cards. If God is your best friend, what can you trade with him? Love? Time? Make a special trading card for God by drawing a picture of something you can give to him or do for him.

Prayer

Thank you for being my best friend, God. Teach me to be a good friend too. Amen.

God Is Easy to Find

You will seek me and find me when you seek me with all your heart.
– Jeremiah 29:13

God's Love

Write "God Loves Me!" on the big heart that covers the earth. Now color the picture.

Prayer

God, thank You for loving me. Teach me to love others better. Amen.

Nothing Is Impossible with God

For with God nothing shall be impossible.
– Luke 1:37 KJV

God Can Do Anything

One spring night, enemy soldiers approached a little town. A family lived in a farmhouse nearby. The young boy in the family often prayed to God. He believed God could do anything.

When the soldiers came near, the boy prayed, "Dear God, please build a wall around this town. Protect us from the enemy soldiers."

The boy's father heard him pray. He said, "Your God can't build a wall around a whole town in one day and night."

The next morning the family woke up to loud claps of thunder and high winds. Large hail fell on the roof. The father could hardly believe his eyes. "Come here, son!" he called. "God has sent a heavy rainstorm. The news reporter said the storm is only over our town. The rain has fallen so much that the soldiers left."

Now the father believes God can do anything. He believes God answers prayers. When God wants to do something for you, no one can stop hHim. God can do anything because his power is awesome.

Your Turn

1. What has God done for you?
2. What kind of power does God have? What kinds of things can he do?

_____

_____

_____

_____

Prayer

Dear God, I am glad you can do anything, and you answer my prayers. Help me trust you and wait for your answers. Thank you. Amen.

Nothing Is Impossible with God

For with God nothing shall be impossible.
– Luke 1:37 KJV

My Impossible List

Think of three things you think are impossible for God to do in your life. Write them on the giant raindrop. Pray each day for them. Remember that God answers prayers with the best for you in mind. God will decide if what you ask for is best for you.

Nothing Is Impossible

1 _____

2 _____

3 _____

Prayer

God, nothing is impossible for you. Sometimes things seem impossible for me. Help me to remember to pray and ask for your help. Amen.

Nothing Is Impossible with God

For with God nothing shall be impossible.
– Luke 1:37 KJV

The Rock

Water flowed out of the rock for Moses and the people. God showed he cared for them by sending water. Think of two ways God shows he cares for you. Write them on the rock.

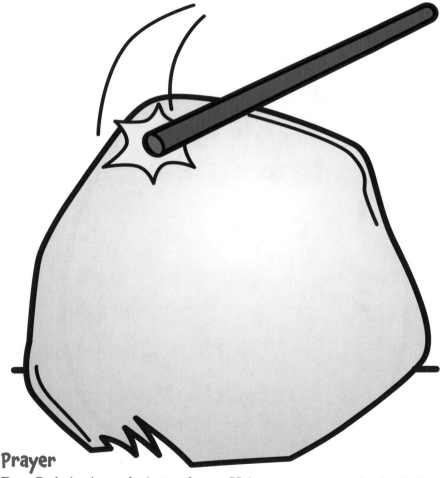

Prayer

Dear God, thank you for loving for me. Help me to see more clearly all the ways you care for me. Amen.

Nothing Is Impossible with God

For with God nothing shall be impossible.
– Luke 1:37 KJV

God Uses His Power to Show His Love

A radio needs power to work. A television takes electric power. An electric train set needs power. A telephone works with power. All of these things run by power invented and harnessed by people.

God is powerful all by himself. He has the power to do anything. The Bible is a great place to find out how God uses his power to help people.

One time God's people were traveling in the desert. The people had nothing to drink. They were very thirsty and didn't know what to do. Moses was their leader. He cried out to God, "What am I to do with these people? They are almost ready to stone me" (Exodus 17:4).

God told Moses to take his walking stick and go ahead of the people. "I will stand there before you by the rock at Horeb," said God. "Strike the rock, and water will come out of it" (Exodus 17:6).

And that is exactly what happened! The people knew God was taking care of them. God still shows his powerful love by caring for people—including you—today.

Your Turn

1. How is God's power different than your power?
   How does God show his power to people today?
2. What other stories in the Bible show God using his power to care for people?

_____

_____

_____

Prayer

Dear God, thank you for your power and might. Let me know you more as I see your power in the Bible and in my life.

Nothing Is Impossible with God

For with God nothing shall be impossible.
– Luke 1:37 KJV

God's Army

Draw a picture on the city wall that shows ways you can help your friends and neighbors get to know God.

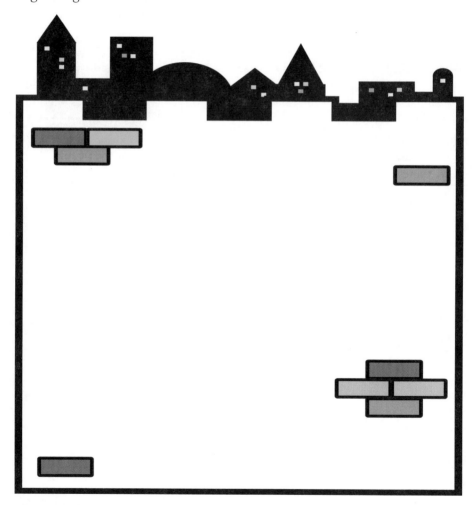

Prayer

Dear God, I pray my friends will want to know you. Help me tell them about you and Jesus. Amen.

Nothing Is Impossible with God

For with God nothing shall be impossible.
– Luke 1:37 KJV

God's Protection

Hebrews 10:22 in the Bible says, "Let us draw near to God with a sincere heart and with the full assurance that faith brings." Draw yourself in a tent or under an umbrella to remember that God protects you.

Prayer

God, I want to be your child and your friend. I know I only have to ask, and you will come into my heart. I love you and I am asking you now. I want to know you! Amen.

Nothing Is Impossible with God

For with God nothing shall be impossible.
– Luke 1:37 KJV

God Is Your Powerful LORD

How does God show his power today? What do you see around you that shows God's power and might? Draw a picture inside the frame of one thing around you that shows God's power.

Prayer

God, help me to know you more each day. Show me your power and love. Amen.

God's Awesome Wonders

Sing praise to him; tell of all his wonderful acts.
– Psalm 105:2

The Sun and Moon Stand Still

Imagine fighting five armies in one battle. That is just what God's army did. God told his general, Joshua, "Don't be afraid. I'll help you win."

Joshua's army marched all night to surprise the five kings and their soldiers. God made the enemy soldiers confused, so they ran away. Big hail stones fell from the sky on top of the enemy.

Joshua prayed to God, "Let the sun stand still." The sun stood still and the moon stopped for one whole day. That gave God's army more daylight to fight the enemy and win.

God's people defeated the kings and their armies. The Bible reveals many other times God helped people who followed him. God is so powerful! You should tell people about your wonderful God. His power helps you and shows you his love.

Your Turn

1. Today who will you tell about God's wonderful power?

2. How does God show his power today?

3. Do you believe God can do anything?

_____

_____

_____

_____

Prayer

Dear God, you are powerful and kind. Thank you for caring about me and using your power to show love to me. Amen.

God's Awesome Wonders

Sing praise to him; tell of all his wonderful acts.
– Psalm 105:2

A Chalkboard Message

Decode this message to discover something true about God.

Prayer

Dear God, thank you for ruling over me. I know I am safe because you are near. Amen.

God's Awesome Wonders

Sing praise to him; tell of all his wonderful acts.
– Psalm 105:2

Prayer Shadows

God sent a sign of his faithfulness to King Hezekiah. The stairs were in a shadow, and God made the shadow back up.

Write three prayers inside the stairs below. When God answers your prayers, record the answers at the bottom of the page.

Prayer

Thank you, God, for hearing my prayers. Please remind me to pray for others.
Amen

God's Awesome Wonders

Sing praise to him; tell of all his wonderful acts.
– Psalm 105:2

God Rules

Jason was a daydreamer at school. He stared at the chalkboard. He looked like he was listening to Mrs. Pack's math lesson, but he wasn't. He was thinking about a Bible story he'd heard. The story was about a king who thought he was more important than God. This king built statues of himself and made the people worship him instead of God.

One night the king invited many people to eat dinner with him. As they ate and drank, something weird happened. A hand appeared by the wall. The fingers began writing. The king was scared. His face went white. His knees were shaking. He called in his magicians and advisors to tell him what the writing said. No one could read the writing. Then the queen said, "Don't be alarmed…Call for Daniel, and he will tell you what the writing means" (Daniel 5:10, 12).

Daniel was called in. He looked at the wall and saw *"MENE, MENE, TEKEL, PARSIN."*

"Read the wall for me," the king ordered.

Daniel said, *"MENE:* God has numbered the days of your reign and brought it to an end. *TEKEL:* You have been weighed on the scales and found wanting. *PARES:* Your kingdom is divided and given to the Medes and Persians" (Daniel 5: 26-28).

That very night the king died and everything happened like Daniel had said. Unlike the king, Daniel let God rule his life.

Your Turn

1. What does it mean to let God rule in your life?

2. Why do you think only Daniel could read the writing?

_____

_____

_____

Prayer

Dear God, I want you to rule in my life always. Amen.

God's Awesome Wonders

Sing praise to him; tell of all his wonderful acts.
– Psalm 105:2

Mail for God

The Bible reveals many times when God sent messages to his people. He speaks to us today through his Word. Draw a picture or write a message to God that thanks him for his power.

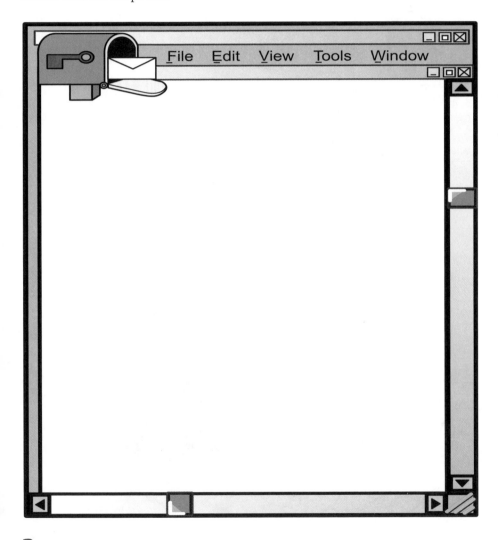

Prayer

Dear God, thank you for giving me the Bible so I will know about your power. Amen.

God's Awesome Wonders

Sing praise to him; tell of all his wonderful acts.
– Psalm 105:2

God Loves You!

Color the footprints that go from your house all the way to God's home in heaven.

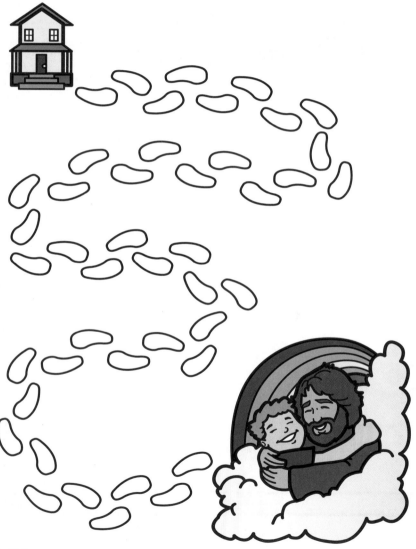

Prayer

Thank you, God, for caring for me and loving me. You are wonderful. Amen.

God's Awesome Wonders

Sing praise to him; tell of all his wonderful acts.
– Psalm 105:2

The Sharing Sandwich

One time Jesus fed thousands of people with five loaves of bread and two fish. Nothing is too hard for God! Make a "sharing sandwich." Draw pictures or write on each part of the sandwich things you can share with your family and friends.

Prayer

Dear God, help me share with others. Show me ways I can help my family and friends. Amen.

Jesus Wants You to Trust Him

Trust in the LORD with all your heart.
– Proverbs 3:5

Water Shoes

Water-skiing is fun. Water skis are like long shoes. They help you slide along on top of the water. When you water ski, you wear a life jacket and hold on to a rope tied to a boat. As the boat moves, the skis and rope pull you up and out of the water. You glide along the top of the water in your water shoes. You trust the boat and the skis to keep you going.

One day Jesus sent his friends out on a boat while he went to pray. It was dark on the lake. A strong wind blew in. From the hills, Jesus saw his friends rowing hard. They were trying to move, but the wind blew the boat the other way. Jesus walked out to them on top of the water. His friends were afraid because they thought he was a ghost.

"Take courage!" said Jesus. "It is I. Don't be afraid" (Matthew 14:27).

Peter wanted to go to Jesus.

"Come," said Jesus.

Peter got out of the boat and stepped onto the water. He walked toward Jesus, but when he saw the waves he got scared. He started to sink. "LORD, save me!"

Jesus reached out and lifted him from the water. Then they climbed into the boat.

Jesus wants you to trust him to love and care for you right where you are.

Your Turn

1. Why did Peter sink?

2. Do you trust Jesus to help you when you're sad or angry?

_____

_____

_____

_____

Prayer

Dear God, help me to trust you at home and at school. Teach me how to keep my eyes on you. Amen.

Jesus Wants You to Trust Him

Trust in the LORD with all your heart.
– Proverbs 3:5

Trust Line

Connect the dots to help the boy reach Jesus. On the lines write down three reasons why you trust Jesus.

Prayer

Dear God, I know that when I pray, I can trust you to listen and answer. Amen.

Jesus Wants You to Trust Him

Trust in the Lord with all your heart.
– Proverbs 3:5

PUSH the Wheelbarrow

P-U-S-H stands for **P**ray **U**ntil **S**omething **H**appens. When you think of PUSH and then choose to pray, big things can happen.

So begin PUSHing and praying! Watch God answer your prayers. Write down some of your prayer requests in the wheelbarrow.

1. _____
   _____
   _____
2. _____
   _____
   _____

Prayer

God, please help me to remember PUSH: **P**ray **U**ntil **S**omething **H**appens. I know big things can happen when I pray. Amen.

46

Jesus Wants You to Trust Him

Trust in the LORD with all your heart.
– Proverbs 3:5

Surprised!

Did you know Jesus surprised his friends once? Peter and some guys decided to go out on the lake to fish. They fished all night, but they didn't catch anything.

Morning came, and a man on shore called, "Friends, haven't you any fish?"

"No!" they shouted back.

"Throw your net on the right side of the boat and you will find some," the man told them (John 21:6).

They threw their net over the right side of the boat. They caught so many fish they had a hard time pulling in the net. Peter counted 153 fish!

There was a campfire when they got to shore. They were very surprised to see the man was Jesus, who had risen from the dead. "Have breakfast!" He said.

Jesus can surprise you too. He is always near even when you aren't looking for Him or paying attention.

Your Turn

1. How did Jesus surprise his friends?

2. How does Jesus surprise you?

_____

_____

_____

_____

Prayer

Thank you, Lord, for your presence. I want to be near you because you make me happy. It makes you happy too! Amen.

Jesus Wants You to Trust Him

Trust in the LORD with all your heart.
– Proverbs 3:5

The Fish Net

Draw a net that connects the fish and the fisherman to remember Jesus will sometimes surprise you with his presence. (See John 21.)

Prayer

Thank you, Lord, that you are always near. I want to be in your presence forever. Amen.

Jesus Wants You to Trust Him

Trust in the LORD with all your heart.
– Proverbs 3:5

Meet Jesus on the Road

When you find out about Jesus and ask him to be Your Lord and Savior, you will be changed. Do you want to meet Jesus? Have you already met Jesus? Meet Jesus on the road. Draw a picture of yourself next to Jesus to show you know him. Write your name on the road sign.

Prayer

Dear Jesus, I know you and I love you. Help me be more like you. Amen.

Jesus Wants You to Trust Him

Trust in the LORD with all your heart.
– Proverbs 3:5

Cloud Drawings

Jesus is in heaven now. Someday he will return to earth in a cloud. That will be a special day for you! Draw a picture of your friends and you meeting Jesus.

Prayer

Dear Jesus, help me to share your love with my friends. Amen.

Follow God

Obey the LORD *your God and*
carefully follow all his commands.
– Deuteronomy 28:1

God Wants to Protect You

On the first day of school, Mr. Clark gave the classroom rules for the students to follow. Phil listened carefully. *"The same rules,"* he thought. *"Every year I hear the same rules."*

"Rules are very important," said Mr. Clark. "Some rules are made so games will be fun and interesting. Other rules help you show respect for others. In soccer, there is a rule that you can't touch the ball with your hands. That makes the game fun. In basketball, no pushing or shoving is allowed. That rule shows respect for others. One football rule says you can't pull on the front of a player's helmet. It's easy to see the reason for that rule."

Phil knew Mr. Clark was right. Rules are made for many good reasons. They help keep people safe. Some rules are created to make life easier.

Did you know God also gives you rules to follow? His rules keep you safe and help you know when you are doing something wrong. Another name for "rule" is "commandment." God gave his people ten special rules that we call "the Ten Commandments." Do you know them? You can find them in the Old Testament of your Bible, in Exodus 20.

Your Turn

1. Why do your parents give you rules to follow?

2. Why does God want you to follow his rules?

_____

_____

Prayer

Thank you, God, for loving me enough to give me rules. You want to protect me. You are a great God! Amen.

Follow God

*Obey the LORD your God and
carefully follow all his commands.*
– Deuteronomy 28:1

Keeping Safe

Think of three rules that God and your parents would like you to follow. Write one rule on each of the balls.

Prayer

Dear God, I know you and my parents have rules for me to follow. I know they are to help me. Thank you for taking such good care of me. Amen.

Follow God

*Obey the LORD your God and
carefully follow all his commands.*
– Deuteronomy 28:1

Pleasing God

Look at the boy. Think of ways he can please God with his hands, feet, heart, lips, eyes, and ears. Write your ideas by the different body parts and remember that you can do these things too. Now have fun coloring the boy.

Prayer

Dear God, I want to remember to please you. Help me think of ways I can make you happy. Amen.

Follow God

*Obey the LORD your God and
carefully follow all his commands.*
– Deuteronomy 28:1

Pleasing God

Don't worry about what Ben thinks of your picture," said John's friend Mike. "You did your best, that's all that matters."

As John added his card to the other homemade birthday cards, he saw that they were all different and nice in their own way. "Well, I did try hard because Mrs. Carol is my favorite teacher. I sure hope she is happy with it," John said.

"I'm sure Mrs. Carol will be happy to get your card," Mike said. "But even if she didn't, doing your best makes God happy."

God's Rules

1. Put God first.
2. Love God most.
3. Honor God's name.
4. Keep Sundays special.
5. Honor your father and mother.
6. Respect and protect life.
7. Be true when you marry.
8. Keep only what is yours.
9. Be honest.
10. Want only what is yours.

Your Turn

1. Why do you want to discover what pleases God?
2. Do these 10 rules sound familiar? Where have you heard them before?

Prayer

Dear God, help me remember what pleases you. I want to make you happy. Amen.

Follow God

*Obey the LORD your God and
carefully follow all his commands.*
– Deuteronomy 28:1

God Is First

Nothing should be more important to you than God. The first rule in the Ten Commandments is to put God first. Use the picture below to find the words for the crossword puzzle. The words in the puzzle are things you might wrongly put before God.

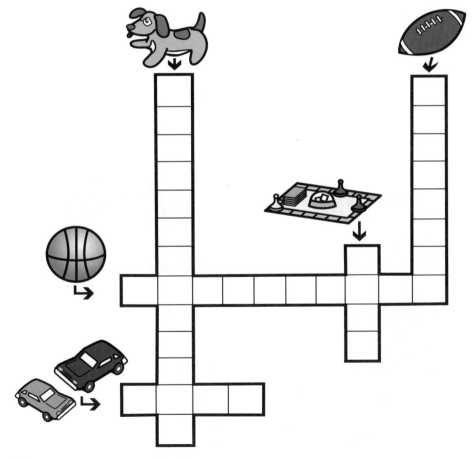

Prayer

God, help me follow your rules. Pleasing you is the best thing I can do. Amen.

Follow God

*Obey the LORD your God and
carefully follow all his commands.*
– Deuteronomy 28:1

A Secret Message

Decode the secret message on the pony's blanket. Every day think of ways you
can do what the message says.

a	b	c	d	e	f	g	h	i
1	2	3	4	5	6	7	8	9

j	k	l	m	n	o	p	q	r
10	11	12	13	14	15	16	17	18

s	t	u	v	w	x	y	z
19	20	21	22	23	24	25	26

$$\overline{16} \ \overline{21} \ \overline{20}$$

$$\overline{7} \ \overline{15} \ \overline{4}$$

$$\overline{6} \ \overline{9} \ \overline{18} \ \overline{19} \ \overline{20}$$

Prayer

Dear God, I am glad you love me. I am sorry when I don't put you first. Thank
you for forgiving me. Amen.

Follow God

*Obey the LORD your God and
carefully follow all his commands.*
– Deuteronomy 28:1

Skating on the Pond

Matthew 12:9-13 tells us that Jesus did good things for people. On the frozen lake, write at least two good things Jesus did on the Sabbath. ("Sabbath" is a day in the week set aside to focus on God and worship him. Many Christians do this on Sunday.) Now write at at least two things you can do to focus on God and help other people.

Prayer

Dear God, help me to always think of you. Show me what I can do to honor you. Amen.

Pleasing God

Live a life worthy of the Lord and please him in every way:
bearing fruit in every good work, growing in the knowledge of God.
– Colossians 1:10

Discovering How to Please

"Vacation is finally here," said Jeff. "No school for two weeks!"

"You won't stop learning because school is out," his dad said. "I know a lesson we can do together!" Jeff's dad grabbed his Bible. He turned to Colossians in the New Testament. Jeff's dad read out loud, "Live a life worthy of the Lord and please him in every way."

"Is that the lesson?" asked Jeff.

"Yes!" answered his dad. "Pleasing God is a good lesson."

"I understand!" Jeff said. "But how do I find out what pleases God?"

"A good place to begin is by reading the Bible just like we are doing now," his dad said. "You can also obey your mom and me. Putting your friends before yourself and helping them also pleases God. Obeying God's Ten Commandments will help you."

"I already try to do those things," said Jeff.

"Great!" Dad said. "Do your mouth, hands, and feet always seek to please God? Do you want to please God more than yourself?"

"I understand what you mean, Dad. I guess I still have a few more things to learn about pleasing God," said Jeff.

"That's my guy!" said his dad as he put his arm around Jeff. "Don't worry. Your mom and I will help you."

Your Turn

1. Why does it sometimes seem like it is hard to please God?
2. Name some ways you can please God with your mouth, hands, and feet.

_____

_____

_____

_____

Prayer

God, help me please you every day. Amen.

Pleasing God

Live a life worthy of the Lord and please him in every way:
bearing fruit in every good work, growing in the knowledge of God.
– Colossians 1:10

Be Honest

Lying is not a good thing to do. God says to be honest. Sometimes it seems easier to lie instead of telling the truth. Don't let your mouth be a trap for lying. Write down rule 9 that you learned from the Ten Commandments. Then color the mouth trap.

Prayer

Dear God, help me to always tell the truth and not hurt anyone with what I say. Amen.

Pleasing God

*Live a life worthy of the Lord and please him in every way:
bearing fruit in every good work, growing in the knowledge of God.*
– Colossians 1:10

Pleasing God

Solve the puzzle to discover what to do every day to please God by using your mouth, feet, and hands.

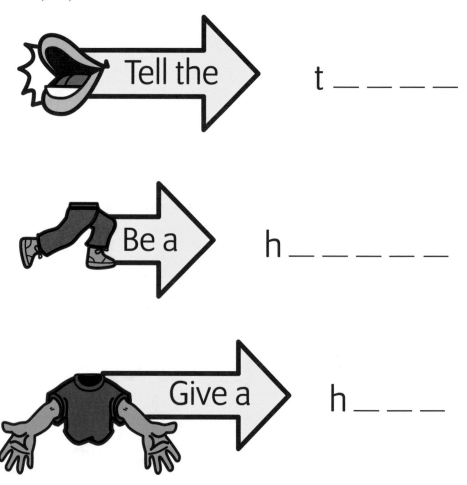

Tell the   t _ _ _ _

Be a   h _ _ _ _ _

Give a   h _ _ _

Prayer

Dear God, I want to use my mouth, feet, and hands—every part of me—to please you. Amen.

Pleasing God

Live a life worthy of the Lord and please him in every way:
bearing fruit in every good work, growing in the knowledge of God.
– Colossians 1:10

Does Your Heart Belong to God?

It is fun to build with blocks. To build a tower, you must find the right size and shape of blocks to stack. The blocks must fit together so the tower will stand without falling over. In a similar way, the pieces of a jigsaw puzzle lock together to make a picture. Each piece is important.

God put 10 important rules together to help you keep them in your heart. Each rule is important to know and think about. God's rules can keep you safe.

The more you follow God's rules, the more you become like Jesus. Keeping the 10 special rules in your heart is like putting a puzzle together and seeing how great it looks.

There is one more very important rule for you to know. It is the greatest rule God gives: "Love the Lord your God with all your heart" (Matthew 22:37).

Your Turn

1. How will "loving the Lord with all your heart" help you follow God's rules?
2. What does God mean when He says to love Him with all your heart?

_____

_____

_____

_____

Prayer

God, thank you for giving me rules to follow and for loving me. Amen.

Pleasing God

Live a life worthy of the Lord and please him in every way:
bearing fruit in every good work, growing in the knowledge of God.
– Colossians 1:10

The Happiness Cage

Exodus 20:17 tells us to not covet. "Covet" means to want something that isn't ours or that we don't need. Here are two cages with a monkey in each one. One of the monkeys has taken as much food as he needs and leaves the rest. The other monkey grabs as much food as he can—more than he can possibly eat. Which monkey would God say is the happiest? Put a smile on the face of the monkey who is content with what he needs. Put a sad face on the monkey who wants more than he needs.

Prayer

Lord, help me not to want everything I see in ads. Show me how to love you and be happy with what I have. Amen.

Pleasing God

Live a life worthy of the Lord and please him in every way:
bearing fruit in every good work, growing in the knowledge of God.
– Colossians 1:10

Puzzle Blocks

Do you remember God's 10 special rules and the most important one? Fill in the missing words on the puzzle blocks.

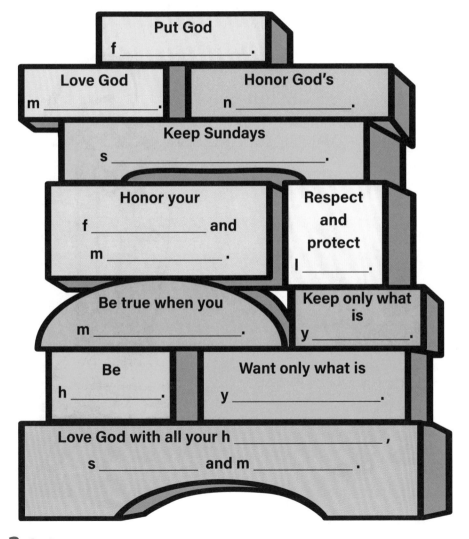

Put God
f _____.

Love God
m _____.

Honor God's
n _____.

Keep Sundays
s _____.

Honor your
f _____ and
m _____.

Respect and protect
l _____.

Be true when you
m _____.

Keep only what is
y _____.

Be
h _____.

Want only what is
y _____.

Love God with all your h _____,
s _____ and m _____.

Prayer

Lord, please help me remember your rules so that I will please you. Amen.

63

Pleasing God

Live a life worthy of the Lord and please him in every way:
bearing fruit in every good work, growing in the knowledge of God.
– Colossians 1:10

Team Player

A "team" is when people work together to accomplish a goal. A family is a team. Many sports depend on teamwork. Working together is good in God's eyes. Draw a picture of yourself on this basketball team to remind yourself that God wants family members and team members to work together and care for each other.

Prayer

Dear God, I want to be on your team! And I want to help my family and friends. Help me be a good team player. Give me friends who love you. Amen.

Keep Your Eyes on Jesus

[Fix] our eyes on Jesus.
– Hebrews 12:2

Look around at everything you see. Your eyes see television shows, video games, movies, sports games, and a lot more. Seeing those things isn't bad. But there's something more important to pay attention to. Jesus wants you to think about Him more than anything else.

Watch Jesus

"Nick, Mrs. Rose needs someone to watch Buffy, her cat," said Nick's mom.

"When?" he asked.

"Tonight. She is going into the hospital for surgery," said Mom.

"Do I have to?" asked Nick. "Ben and I want to play basketball after school. I don't have time to help."

"You can play basketball with Ben any day," said Nick's mom. "Helping Mrs. Rose will be like helping Jesus. When your eyes are on Jesus, you will want to help others. Jesus helped people, and he wants you to do that too."

Nick thought about that. "You are right, Mom. I will come home after school and help Mrs. Rose. I want to be like Jesus!"

Your Turn

1. Is there someone God wants you to help today?
2. How do you feel when your eyes and mind are focused on Jesus?

_____

_____

_____

Prayer

God, I want to be ready to help people all the time. Show me someone I can help today. Help me keep my eyes on you. Amen.

Keep Your Eyes on Jesus

[Fix] our eyes on Jesus.
– Hebrews 12:2

God's Child

Are you a child of God? If not, do you want to be? John 1:12 says, "Those who believe in [Jesus's] name, he gave the right to become children of God." Do you believe in Jesus? Fill in the missing letters and then color Jesus and the boy.

To th__se wh__
b__lie__e in
(Jesus') n__me,
He g__ve t__e
r__ght t__
be__om__
chi__dr__n
__f Go__.
~ John 1:12

Prayer

Dear God, I want to be one of your children. I know that loving you means trying to do everything in ways that will please you. Help me do things your way. Amen.

Keep Your Eyes on Jesus

[Fix] our eyes on Jesus.
– Hebrews 12:2

Getting a Clean Heart

All people make mistakes, even God's children. When we accept Jesus as savior and are baptized, all of the mistakes we made or will make, are washed away (Acts 22:16). So the good news is when you make a mistake, you can tell God you are sorry and ask him to forgive you. And he will!

Look at the T-shirts below. Each one is labeled with a mistake. When Jesus forgives you, it's like making the dirty T-shirt clean and white. Clean up your life and heart by telling God you are sorry and ask him to forgive you.

Color over the T-shirts with white out to show that your mistakes are wiped away and you are clean. Remember—only Jesus can wipe your heart completely clean.

Prayer

Dear God, the Bible says you will wash my mistakes away and I will be so clean my heart will be whiter than snow. Please forgive me for doing wrong. I am so glad you will make me clean again. Amen.

Keep Your Eyes on Jesus

[Fix] our eyes on Jesus.
– Hebrews 12:2

God's Child

Grant's brother had to have 10 stitches to close a gash on his head. They had gotten into a fight, and Grant hit him with a tennis racket. At school, Grant threw spitballs on the wall and was sent him to the principal's office. Grant told his parents and the principal that he didn't have to obey them.

The children's pastor at church talked to Grant. The pastor said, "Do you believe Jesus died for you? Do you know he loves you?"

"Of course. I go to church, and my parents are Christians," Grant said.

"Going to church and having parents who love Jesus doesn't make you a child of God," explained the pastor. "Every person must personally decide to follow Jesus. He must love Jesus and want to follow his ways. He wants to please God by following his rules. Do you want that?"

"Yes. I am sorry for causing trouble," Grant admitted. "I love Jesus and want to follow him."

"Let's pray together," said the pastor. "We will ask God to help you follow his rules."

Your Turn

1. Grant went to church and his parents knew Jesus. Did that mean Grant was a Christian?
2. Are you God's child?

_____

_____

_____

Prayer

Dear God, I want to be your child and follow you. I want to do things your way from now on. Amen.

Keep Your Eyes on Jesus

[Fix] our eyes on Jesus.
– Hebrews 12:2

God's Hands

No matter how strong you are, it can be hard to always do the right thing. The Bible says you can do all things when you ask Jesus to help you. Under Jesus's hand, write down three things you have a hard time with. Now ask Jesus to help you.

Prayer

Dear God, I know that with your help I can do anything. With your help, I can be who you want me to be. Amen.

Keep Your Eyes on Jesus

[Fix] our eyes on Jesus.
– Hebrews 12:2

Police Scramble?

The police help keep you safe when you ask for their help. God will help you even more when you ask him for help.

Break the code to find an exciting promise from God. See the letters and numbers in the raindrops? Use the numbers to put each letter in the right order on the lines below the police car.

$$\overline{}_1 \quad \overline{}_2 \overline{}_3 \overline{}_4 \overline{}_5 \quad \overline{}_6 \overline{}_7 \overline{}_8$$

$$\overline{}_9 \overline{}_{10} \overline{}_{11} \overline{}_{12} \overline{}_{13} \overline{}_{14} \quad \overline{}_{15} \overline{}_{16} \overline{}_{17}!$$

Prayer

Dear God, I want to trust you all the time but sometimes I forget. Forgive me for not asking you for help. I am so happy you will never forget me. Amen.

Keep Your Eyes on Jesus

[Fix] our eyes on Jesus.
– Hebrews 12:2

One way to keep your eyes on Jesus is by knowing the Bible. Here are two great Bible verses. To help you remember them, do two things. First write each verse three times. Then say the verses out loud to your parents every day until you have them memorized.

"Let us fix our eyes on Jesus" (Hebrews 12:2).

_____

_____

_____

_____

_____

"I can do everything through Him who gives me strength" (Philippians 4:13).

_____

_____

_____

_____

_____

Prayer

Lord, I want to fix my eyes on you. Help me read my Bible and obey you. Amen.

Do What Is Right

Never tire of doing what is good.
– 2 Thessalonians 3:13

The Grumpy Man

Tim slid into the van after school.

"Hi, buddy!" his mom said. "How was your day?"

"Not so hot," answered Tim.

Mom turned toward him. "Why the long face?"

Tim said, "Grumpy Mr. Martin, the lunch room aide, got mad at me today. He said Tony and I were throwing food, but we weren't. It was Jason. We weren't doing anything wrong. We were just eating our lunches."

"Sometimes adults make mistakes," Tim's mom said.

"Do you think Mr. Martin is a happy person?" asked Tim.

"He doesn't look happy," answered Mom. "You can usually tell when people are happy on the inside because they smile on the outside. But only God knows what is in a person's heart. The Bible says in Psalm 4:7 that God filled David's heart with joy. David knew God, and that's what made him happy inside and out."

Tim thought for a minute. "Maybe Mr. Martin doesn't know God and his love. I am going to pray for him."

Your Turn

1. Everyone gets grumpy sometimes. What makes you grumpy?
2. Why does being happy on the inside make you smile on the outside?

_____

_____

_____

_____

Prayer

God, help me to know you better every day. I want to know more about your love for me and how I can love you. Amen.

Do What Is Right

Never tire of doing what is good.

– 2 Thessalonians 3:13

Happy or Sad Face

Knowing and thinking about God makes a person smile. Draw a happy face below the pictures showing boys who are happy. Draw a sad face below the pictures showing boys who are sad.

Prayer

God, knowing you makes me happy. And because I am happy, I want to tell my friends about you. Amen.

Do What Is Right

Never tire of doing what is good.
– 2 Thessalonians 3:13

Greatness Hoop

Being great for God means doing something that helps people and shows God's love. You can be great for God! Beside each basketball, write one way you will be great for God at home, at school, and at church.

Prayer

Dear God, I am glad I know you. Help me keep my eyes on you. I want to be great for you so people will want to know you. Amen.

Do What Is Right

Never tire of doing what is good.
– 2 Thessalonians 3:13

The Right Circle

The first time Dave played Twister with his sister, he lost. With every turn, Dave's arms and legs twisted around hers. Pretty soon he lost his balance and fell on the mat. Do you sometimes feel like you've fallen flat on your face? If you make a mistake or don't go the right way, you can end up doing wrong things.

Preston went to the store. He wanted some candy, but he didn't have enough money. He saw that the store clerk was on the phone. Preston thought he could probably steal the candy without getting caught.

It was like Preston was on one of those colored circles on the Twister mat and ready to move. If he moved one way and walked out of the store, he would please God. If he moved a different way and stole the candy, he would do wrong. God wouldn't be pleased, and Preston might get caught. Preston didn't take the candy. He kept his eyes on God and remained on the right path.

Your Turn

1. Why was it important for Dave to stay on the right circle?
2. What can happen when we choose not to follow and obey God?
3. How does the Bible help you go the right way?

_____

_____

_____

_____

Prayer

God, help me understand how to do what's right. When I do wrong, put me back on the right path. Amen.

Do What Is Right

Never tire of doing what is good.

– 2 Thessalonians 3:13

Pleasing God

Look at the words in the circles. Color the circles that list the right thing to do. Cross out the circles that list activities that would not be pleasing to God.

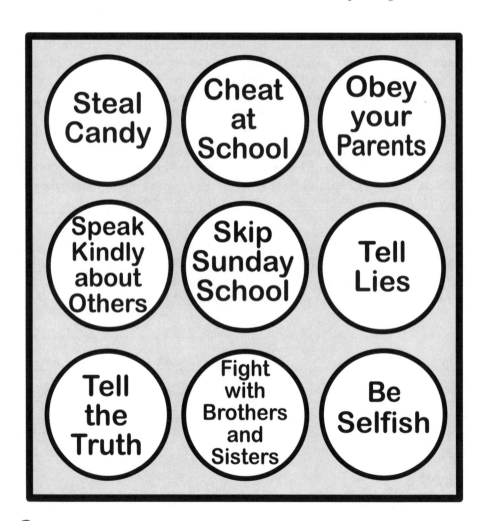

Prayer

Dear God, help me to never tire of doing right. I want to go the right way— your way! Amen.

Do What Is Right

Never tire of doing what is good.

– 2 Thessalonians 3:13

Jesus Globe

God wants us to change our world for Jesus. On the space below, write three things you can do to help change your world at home, school, and in your neighborhood.

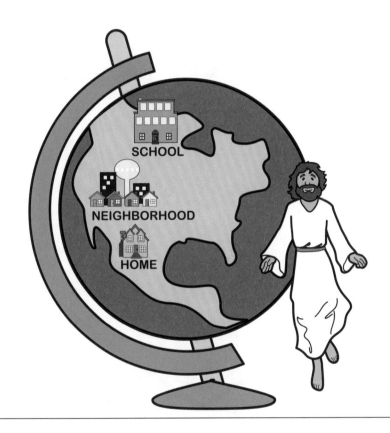

_____

_____

_____

Prayer

God, thank you for loving me so I can be a world changer. Show me how I can change the world for you. Amen.

Do What Is Right

Never tire of doing what is good.
– 2 Thessalonians 3:13

Knowing God's Heart

Draw a picture of yourself inside the heart. On the lines below, list the names of kids you don't know very well. This week call some people on on your list and invite them to your house after school or on a weekend. (Make sure you ask your mom and dad first.)

_____

_____

_____

Prayer

God, you know all about me. I want to know all about you. Please help me get to know you better. Amen.

God Wants You!

The ways of the LORD are right.
– Hosea 14:9

Following God

If you play an instrument or ever heard a singer sing or musician play off key, you know that it's important to perform a song the right way. If it is not, the music will sound a little off. God is like a composer and we are like the musicians. When we decide not to follow God's rules for right living, our lives will feel a little off. If you play video or board games, you know that it's important to follow the rules and play the game in the right way or it can get very confusing and stop being fun. God wants you to follow him and his ways so your life will be as he intended—a life of peace and joy. You can learn about God's ways by reading the Bible and you can follow him by doing what the Bible tells you to do, and talking to God and asking him for help.

You follow a map when you want to go somewhere. The road signs on the map tell you where to go. As you get to know God, he shows you the right way to go. Reading the Bible and talking to God through prayer will help you know his ways. Sometimes life could be unfair but you can always have the peace and joy that come from following God and his ways, and trust that things will work out for you.

Your Turn

1. What happens when you play a game and people don't follow the rules?
2. What are some good things that could happen when you choose to follow God's ways instead of your own?

1. Its not fun

2. You could be happy

Prayer

God, help me follow you at school, at home, and at church. Show me how to follow you so I can live your way. Amen.

God Wants You!

The ways of the Lord are right.

– Hosea 14:9

The Goodness Headlines

Make up a news story headline by filling in the blanks. Think of ways you can show the goodness of God to others. Write down what you are doing or plan to do to show goodness to others.

Daily Herald

Matthew Jones
(your name)

DID NOT GROW WEARY OF DOING GOOD.

HE made the world

AND sent Jes down

Prayer

Jesus, I want to spread your goodness to those around me. Please help me do that. Amen.

God Wants You!

The ways of the Lord are right.

– Hosea 14:9

God's Road Map

Following God's way is like following a good map and taking the right roads to get you to the right place. Write on the street signs ways you can follow God at school and at home. For example, one might be reading your Bible or sharing God's ten special rules.

Prayer

God, the Bible is like a road map for following you. Help me read my Bible daily so I will know the right direction to go. Thank you for your Word. Amen.

God Wants You!

The ways of the LORD are right.
– Hosea 14:9

A Good Job!

Jerry was responsible for taking the evening newspaper to 30 of his neighbors each day. He was careful not to throw the papers into the bushes or far from the porches. Most of the other paperboys and papergirls threw their papers from a moving car or bicycle. Their papers landed on the driveways or on the grass.

Jerry wanted to do a good job. His parents always told him to do his work as if he were doing it for Jesus. Folding 30 papers after school each day was hard. He even had to put a rubber band around each one. When it rained he had to also place the newspapers into bags. Jerry was tired some days. On cold, snowy days he put on his boots. He would march in deep snow to get papers to his neighbors.

The neighbors didn't thank Jerry for doing such a good job. They didn't notice his goodness. But Jerry never gave up. He never got tired of doing good for others and God.

Would Jesus ever get tired of doing good for you? When you disobey him, Jesus forgives and helps you. Jesus never tires of doing good things. He never gets tired of loving you.

Your Turn

1. What can you do when you get tired of doing good?
2. How do you think Jesus feels about the way Jerry works?

1. Never give up
2. Avery proud

Prayer

Jesus, thank you for not getting tired of loving me. Help me to do good to others and to obey you. Help me notice your goodness. Amen.

God Wants You!

The ways of the Lord are right.
– Hosea 14:99

The Ark of Thankfulness

God loves a thankful heart. In the circles on the ark, draw pictures of things you are thankful for.

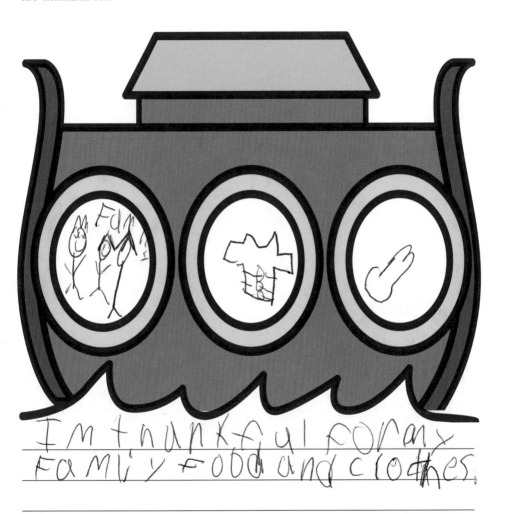

I'm thankful for my family food and clothes

Prayer

God, no matter what's going on in my life, I want to always have a thankful heart. Help me remember to praise you because you are good. Amen.

God Wants You!

The ways of the Lord are right.

– Hosea 14:9

A Thank-You Note to God

God's ways are always right. Write a note to God thanking him for something new he has done for you.

Prayer

God, every day I want to remember to thank you for your goodness to me. Amen.

God Wants You!

The ways of the Lord are right.
– Hosea 14:9

The Goodness Well

The Bible says to trust in the Lord and do good. Think of people you can show
kindness to this week. Write their names and what you will do for them on the
lines next to the well.

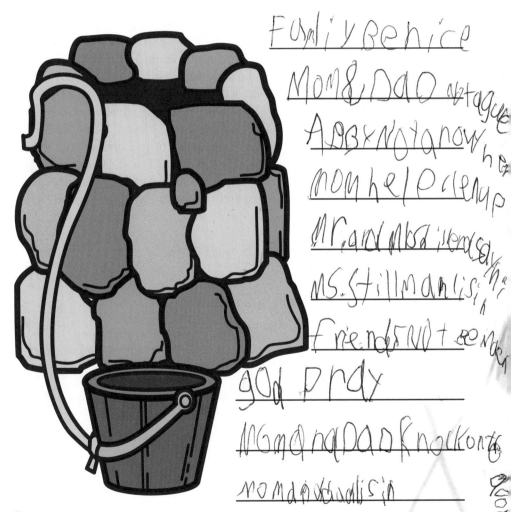

Prayer

God, show me how to do good to others. Help me to do good so that others
will want to do good, too. Amen.

85

God Loves Faithfulness

Teach me your way, O LORD; lead me in a straight path.
– Psalm 27:11

Moses, a Faithful Hero

God gave Moses important jobs because he knew Moses would be faithful. Moses was faithful because he knew God would always help him.

Sometimes it is not easy to do what God wants. God's people were being forced to work for the Egyptians, so God told Moses, "I am sending you to Pharaoh to bring my people the Israelites out of Egypt" (Exodus 3:10).

Moses didn't want to go. "Who am I that I should go to Pharaoh?" Moses was afraid. God knew he would help Moses sway the Pharaoh. God asked Moses, "What is that in your hand?" Moses replied, "A staff." God told Moses to throw his staff on the ground, and it immediately turned into a snake. When Moses picked the snake up by the tail, it became a staff again (Exodus 4:2-4).

Moses was faithful to use the staff each time God told him to. Another time Moses placed the tip of it in the river, and the water turned into blood. After Moses did everything God said to do, the Pharaoh knew God was powerful, so he let the slaves go.

Moses was a hero of God because he was faithful.

Your Turn

1. Why was Moses a faithful hero in God's eyes?
2. How can you be a faithful hero for God?

Becase god wou d all ways help him, Thank him.

Prayer

Lord, help me be faithful to you like Moses was. I want to always do what You and my parents ask me to do. Amen.

God Loves Faithfulness

Teach me your way, O LORD; lead me in a straight path.
– Psalm 27:11

A Faithful Staff

Another name for a walking stick is "staff." Draw a staff in the boy's hand to remind you to always be faithful to God. At the side of the page, write something you can be faithful to do for God.

pray
Be kind
Be prasent
Be helpful
have fun
lisen
Be humbule
Think before you speak

Prayer

God, please help me be faithful to you and obey your rules. Thank you. Amen.

God Loves Faithfulness

Teach me your way, O LORD; lead me in a straight path.
– Psalm 27:11

The Sports Shirt

This boy is playing soccer. What is a way you can show you are faithful to God? Draw it on his shirt.

Prayer

God, I want to be a faithful boy for you. Help me stay on your path. Amen.

God Loves Faithfulness

Teach me your way, O LORD; lead me in a straight path.
– Psalm 27:11

A Faithful Player

"It's too bad Nick is leaving basketball. He is the greatest player that ever lived," Mitch told his dad and brother Alec. Mitch was reading a news story about the basketball player. "It says Nick never missed a game. The players and coaches describe him as being a very hard and committed worker."

"God honors a faithful man," said Dad. "You guys know Nick Justin believes in Jesus, don't you? He often mentions his faith during interviews."

"Wow! I forgot about that," said Mitch. "That explains why I have never seen him arguing with the referee."

"God has blessed Nick because he is faithful," said Dad.

You don't have to be a famous basketball player to be faithful to God. You can be true to him anytime and anywhere. Being faithful to God means obeying your parents when they tell you to clean your room. Being faithful means playing fairly on the playground at school. Sharing and being kind are part of being faithful. Are you a faithful player?

Your Turn

1. Can you think of ways to be a faithful player for God?
2. Look up the word "faithful" in the dictionary. What does it mean?

Not cheat.

Do what he saes. and be Lord,

Prayer

God, make me a faithful kid. Help me do my best in all I do. Keep me faithful to you as I do my chores and love my family. Amen.

God Loves Faithfulness

Teach me your way, O LORD; lead me in a straight path.
– Psalm 27:11

Leading Feet

Did you know God wants faithful people to be leaders? Write your name on each footstep that leads to good behavior. "Jump over" the feet that do not lead to good behavior.

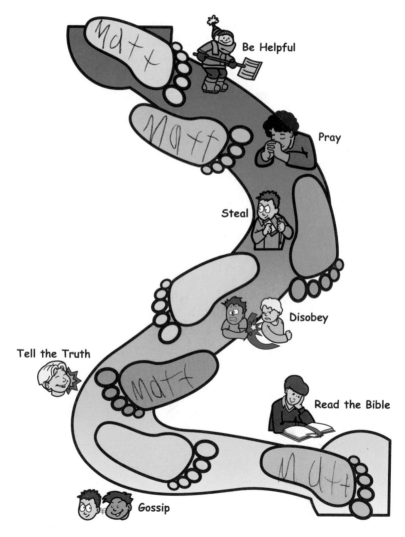

Prayer

God, I want to be a leader for you. Please help me walk in a way that honors you. Amen.

God Loves Faithfulness

Teach me your way, O LORD; lead me in a straight path.
– Psalm 27:11

A Brave Heart

The Bible has many stories of brave men of God. Color the warrior and write inside the heart something you want to be braver in doing.

Prayer

God, help me to have a brave heart for you. Help me to show I am brave because I know you. Amen.

God Loves Faithfulness

Teach me your way, O Lord; lead me in a straight path.
– Psalm 27:11

Adventure Park Slide

Draw a line down the slide to help the brave boy get to the bottom.

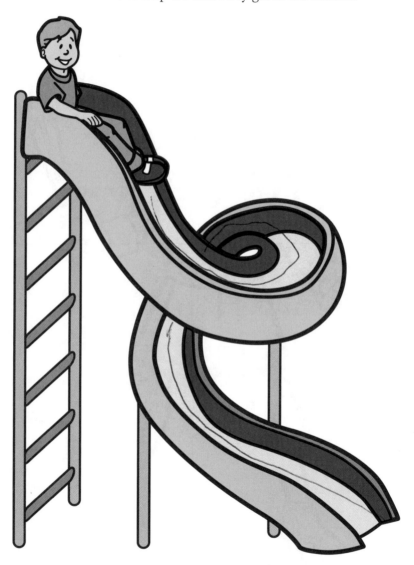

Prayer

God, when I am scared or nervous, I will ask you to help me be brave. Amen.

Willing Workers Wanted

Serve [the LORD] with all your heart and all your soul.
– Joshua 22:5

A Night Call

"Samuel! Samuel!" Samuel was used to Eli, the priest, calling him. He ran to where Eli was sleeping, woke him up, and asked, "You called me?"

"I didn't call; go back and lie down," said Eli.

Samuel went back to bed, but soon he heard, "Samuel!" He got up again and went to Eli. "Here I am; you called me."

Suddenly Eli realized God was calling Samuel. He told Samuel that if he heard God call again, he should say, "Speak, LORD, for your servant is listening" (1 Samuel 3:9).

So Samuel went back to bed. It wasn't long before God said, "Samuel!"

"Speak, for your servant is listening," the boy replied.

God said He was going to surprise people. He was going to judge Eli's family. Eli knew his boys were doing wrong but didn't stop them.

The next morning, Eli asked what God had said.

Samuel was afraid to tell Eli because it was bad news.

"Do not hide [God's words] from me," Eli ordered.

Samuel told Eli what God had said.

Eli said, "He is the LORD; let him do what is good in his eyes."

Samuel was glad God talked to him. God continued to tell him things to pass on to his people.

Your Turn

1. Would you be scared if you heard God calling you?
2. Do you think you might hear God's voice the way Samuel did?

1. Yes
2. I might

Prayer

God, help me hear your voice and then obey what you say. Amen.

Willing Workers Wanted

Serve [the LORD] with all your heart and all your soul.
– Joshua 22:5

Answering God

All through the Bible, we see God calling his people to serve him like Abraham, Moses and Samuel. Read Genesis 22:11, Exodus 3:4, and 1 Samual 3:10. In the space below, write down 1) Abraham, Moses, and Samual's 3-word response, and 2) how you will respond when calls you and tells you to do something?

(your name) Matt
My answer to God: I will
Respod to him and
Do what he says

Prayer

Lord, I want to be like Samuel and hear your voice. Amen.

Willing Workers Wanted

Serve [the LORD] with all your heart and all your soul.
– Joshua 22:5

Baseball Travel

Write your name on home base. Then travel around the bases and write down three things that might keep you from hearing God's voice.

Prayer

Jesus, you are the Lord of my life. I want to listen to you. Please help me stay away from things that keep me from listening to you. Amen.

Willing Workers Wanted

Serve [the LORD] with all your heart and all your soul.
–Joshua 22:5

David Worshipped God

David was one of the greatest kings to rule God's people. God gave him the gift of music. As a shepherd boy, David would sing to his sheep as he watched over them. He also played the harp.

King Saul invited him to his court to play for him. David played and sang, and it soothed the king.

David loved God so much that he wanted to sing. The joy he felt for God made him want to dance too. Through the years, David wrote 73 songs to God. These songs were called "psalms." These psalms are in the Bible.

David's trust in God made him want to worship him. Worshipping God is saying you love him. When David worshipped God, he told him that he was kind, loving, forgiving, and caring. David lifted his hands to the sky and told God he loved him.

Worshipping God is thanking him and loving him. Some people worship God while listening to music. You can worship God anywhere and anytime.

Your Turn

1. Read Psalm 23 in the Bible. What does David call the Lord?
2. Why did David want to worship God?

_____

_____

_____

Prayer

Jesus, you are my God. I worship you and thank you for caring for me. Thank you for being my Shepherd. I don't need anything else when I have you. Amen.

Willing Workers Wanted

Serve [the LORD] with all your heart and all your soul.
– Joshua 22:5

your Psalm to God

On the music paper, write your own psalm or song to God. When you worship him, you can sing or say your psalm to him.

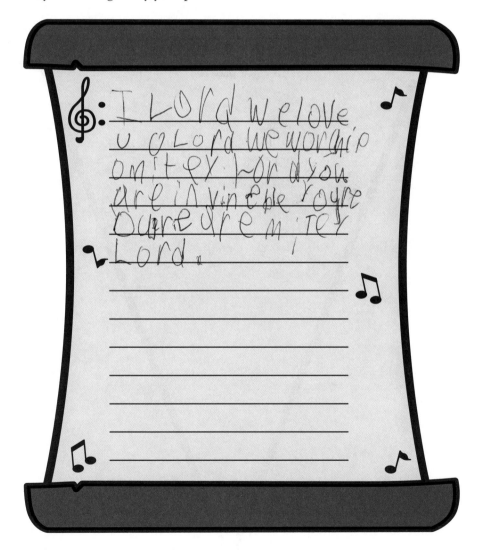

Prayer

God, I want to worship you because you are so great. Help me sing to you every day. Amen.

Willing Workers Wanted

Serve [the LORD] with all your heart and all your soul.
– Joshua 22:5

God's Banner

Draw something on the banner that reminds you of God. Then color the banner and praise God.

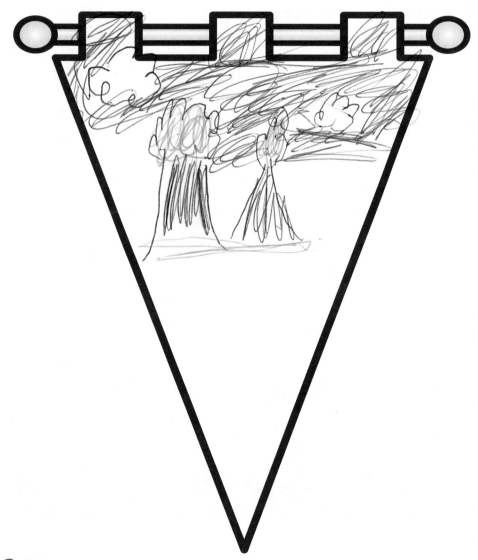

Prayer

I love you, God. I am glad I can worship you. Amen.

Willing Workers Wanted

Serve [the LORD] with all your heart and all your soul.
– Joshua 22:55

God's House

A church is sometimes called "the house of God" or "God's Temple." Draw a house of God around the boy praying.

Prayer

Dear God, when I go to church, I am in your temple. I like going to church to learn about you. I know you hear my prayers wherever I am. Thank you. Amen.

Jesus Is the Best Hero!

There is but one Lord, Jesus Christ.
– 1 Corinthians 8:6

Heroes

"Who is your favorite superhero?" asked Kevin's Sunday school teacher.

"Superman!" called Kevin.

"Jesus is mine," said Brittany.

"Is he like Superman with long hair and a beard?" asked Kevin.

"No, he's nothing like that," replied Brittany. "Superman is fun to watch, but he isn't real. Jesus is real."

"Superman fights crime and gets the bad guys," said Kevin.

"Jesus is real and lives in heaven with God, his Father," she said. "Jesus is kind and loving to all people. It doesn't matter how they look or where they live, he loves them. Jesus fights with truth, not his feet or fists."

"What else do you know about this hero named Jesus?" asked Kevin.

"He is sad when we do wrong, but he is ready to forgive when we are sorry," Brittany replied.

The teacher told Kevin, "Jesus wants to be your number one hero. Jesus came to earth and died to pay for the wrong things we do. God brought Jesus back to life, so now Jesus lives forever. You can make him your hero by loving him and following him."

"I guess Superman isn't my favorite hero after all," Kevin decided.

Your Turn

1. What makes Jesus the best hero ever?

2. Do you want Jesus to be your hero? Pray and ask him!

1. He Died on the cross and came Back to

2. yes I Do!

Prayer

God, thank you for Jesus. Help me to look to him to be my best hero. Amen.

Jesus Is the Best Hero!

There is but one Lord, Jesus Christ.
– 1 Corinthians 8:6

Jesus Says

Instead of playing "Simon Says," play "Jesus Says." Draw a line from the boy to the pictures that show people copying Jesus. Put an X over the pictures that don't copy Jesus.

Prayer

Jesus, help me copy your ways so I know I am doing right. Amen.

Jesus Is the Best Hero!

There is but one Lord, Jesus Christ.
– 1 Corinthians 8:6

The Roller Coaster

Let your friends go first on the roller coaster. Find and circle each word of the question, "What would Jesus do?

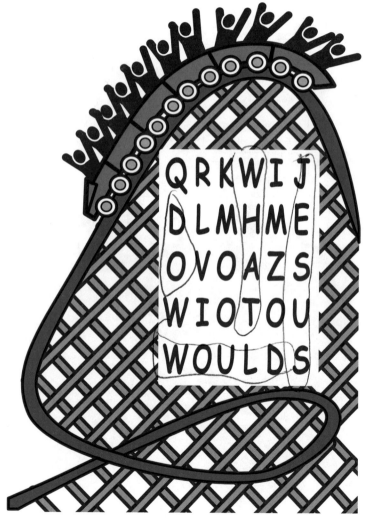

Prayer

Dear Jesus, help me remember to put other people before me. And teach me to always put you first. Amen.

Jesus Is the Best Hero!

There is but one Lord, Jesus Christ.
– 1 Corinthians 8:6

Copying Jesus

Have you ever been called a copycat? A copycat is someone who does something just like someone else.

The Bible says Jesus did good things. Wherever Jesus went, he helped people. Wherever you go, you can do good too. You can copy Jesus! Jesus healed the sick. You can pray and ask God to heal a sick person. You can cheer up someone who is sad. Jesus gave hungry people something to eat. You can help feed people who are hungry. Jesus helped people learn about God. You can talk to children and grownups about God and Jesus. Is there someone you can invite to church today?

Your Turn

1. What are some good things Jesus did?
2. What can you do to copy Jesus?

_____

_____

_____

_____

_____

_____

Prayer

Jesus, I want to be like you. Help me. Amen.

Jesus Is the Best Hero!

There is but one Lord, Jesus Christ.
– 1 Corinthians 8:6

Sand Prints

When you do what Jesus would do, you are following in his steps. Follow Jesus's steps and color each footprint that says something Jesus would do. Skip over the ones Jesus would avoid.

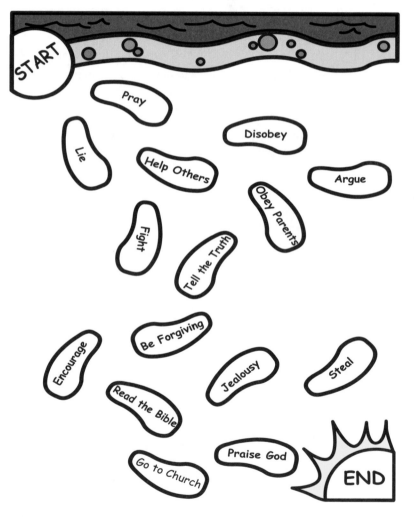

Prayer

Dear Jesus, thank you for your good example. Help me to follow you. Show me how to walk in your steps. Amen.

Jesus Is the Best Hero!

There is but one Lord, Jesus Christ.
– 1 Corinthians 8:6

The Fishing Net

Jesus said, "I will make you fishers of men." He wants you to tell others about him. Draw yourself inside the boat. Fill the net next to the boat by coloring the fish as a reminder to obey Jesus.

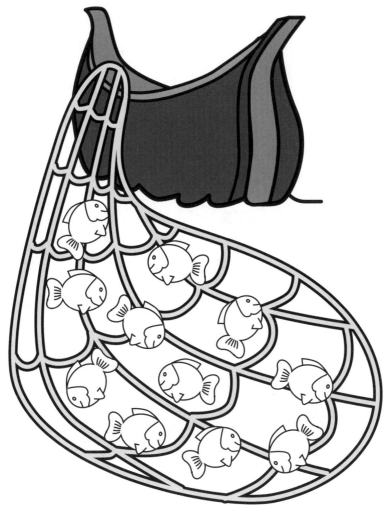

Prayer

Jesus, I pray you will help me obey and follow you. Show me how I can tell others about you. Amen.

Jesus Is the Best Hero!

There is but one Lord, Jesus Christ.
– 1 Corinthians 8:6

Happy at Work

Color each chore item. Draw a happy face on each one to help you remember to be glad when you serve the LORD at home.

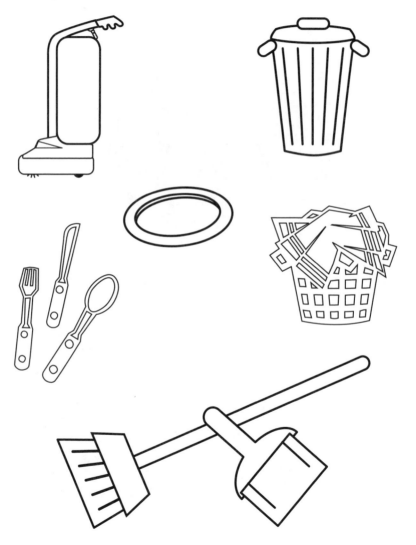

Prayer

Jesus, I am glad you are my Lord and Savior. Help me serve you in whatever I do. Let my work for you be done gladly. Amen.

God Provides the Tools

Keep hold of the deep truths of the faith.
– 1 Timothy 3:9

God's Building Plans

Have you ever built anything? Building a model plane or a birdhouse takes blueprints or plans. The Bible is full of God's building plans that tell you how to create and do good things.

Casey Conner's dad was a furniture builder. The Conners had a woodshop in a separate garage near their home. Casey loved working with his dad in the shop. He enjoyed trying out the many tools his dad stored above a giant workbench. Mr. Conner was an expert builder, and Casey was his trainee.

God is your expert Builder, and you are his trainee. Like Mr. Conner, God keeps tools on hand. He gives you the best tools for building your heart and life his way. His tools include the Bible, faith, love, prayer, service, the Holy Spirit, and even people. Second Peter 1:3 says that, God's "divine power has given us everything we need for a godly life." That means through God's powerful tools you have everything you need to live for him. Work with God—the expert builder. You will enjoy it.

Your Turn

1. Name some of God's tools.
2. How are God's tools used?

_____

_____

_____

_____

Prayer

God, I want you to be my expert builder. Teach me to use your tools to live life the right way. Help me love you more and work with you each day. Amen.

God Provides the Tools

Keep hold of the deep truths of the faith.
– 1 Timothy 3:9

Deep Water

This boy is about to go swimming. He's going to jump into the deep part of the lake. One way you can go deeper with God is to study the Bible. Read the verse at the bottom of the lake. Jesus is the Gate! Think about this and ask God to show you something special from that verse. Write down what the verse means to you.

"I am the gate; whoever enters through me will be saved." John 10:9

Prayer

God, I want to know you better. Please help me dig for deep truths in your Word. Amen.

God Provides the Tools

Keep hold of the deep truths of the faith.
– 1 Timothy 3:9

Your Workbench

God gives you the tools you need to live life for him. Draw workshop tools on the workbench. Ask God in prayer to give you his tools to live life his way.

His divine power has given us everything we need for life and godliness.
2 Peter 1:3

Prayer

Lord, because of your powerful tools, I have everything I need to live correctly. Thank you for giving them to me. Amen.

God Provides the Tools

Keep hold of the deep truths of the faith.
– 1 Timothy 3:9

Fishing for Truth

Peter spent all night fishing on the Sea of Galilee without catching anything (Luke 5:1-11). He was tired of working for nothing and decided to call it quits.

The next day, Jesus got into Peter's boat. After preaching to a small crowd, Jesus told Peter to "take the boat into deeper water and let down your nets for a catch."

Peter thought Jesus was crazy. After fishing all night without catching anything, why would there be fish now? But Peter did as Jesus said. He took the boat into deeper water and fished. Jesus performed a miracle, and Peter caught so many fish that his boat almost sank. When they got to shore, Peter was so impressed by Jesus that he left everything and went with him.

You probably go to Sunday school, you pray, and you try hard to obey the rules. God wants you to be serious about knowing him and his ways. Doing easy things is like fishing in shallow water. Going out into the deep water means working hard to know God and living as a Christian. Take your boat into deep water. Jesus will bless your efforts.

Your Turn

1. Have you ever played it safe and fished in shallow water like Peter did?
2. What is a way you can learn more about Jesus and his ways today?

_____

_____

_____

Prayer

God, I want to know you more. I want to do right and spend more time thinking about you. Teach me to know you better. Amen.

God Provides the Tools

Keep hold of the deep truths of the faith.
– 1 Timothy 3:9

Faith Trail

Have you ever emailed someone or sent a text message to them? When you hit send, you trust the computer or phone to deliver it. You have faith that the message will go where you wanted. Write your name and a short message to God on the email below.

FROM: **TO:**
SUBJECT:

Hello...

Prayer

God, I want to put myself in your hands and give my life completely to you. Thank you for loving me enough to send Jesus to die for me. Amen.

God Provides the Tools

Keep hold of the deep truths of the faith.
– 1 Timothy 3:9

The Sin Bucket

Sin is when you do something God doesn't want you to do. God wants you to get rid of the sins in your life. In the bucket write down those sins you Jesus to help you with.

Prayer

Jesus, thank you for loving me and dying for me on the cross. Teach me to love you back. Amen.

God Provides the Tools

Keep hold of the deep truths of the faith.
– 1 Timothy 3:9

Your Planner

God wants you to be careful what you watch and play. Choose TV programs and video games wisely. With your parents' help, in the guide below, write the TV programs and games that are okay for you to watch and play.

DAY	8am	9am	10am	11am	12pm	1pm	2pm	3pm	4pm	5pm	6pm	7pm	8pm	9pm	Program and Game Titles

My TV and Game Plan

Prayer

Lord, I know you want me to be careful about what I look at. Teach me to watch programs and play games that reflect your teachings. Amen.

How to Pray God's Way

Our Father in heaven, hallowed be your name...
– Matthew 6:9

Praising God's Name

Calvin loved going to his brother Sam's football games at the high school. Everyone in their small town knew Sam because he was the star player. Calvin loved watching and cheering for his brother's team. And he could tell people were proud of his brother too. They often talked about what a good player he was. "He is quick and can run very fast" and "There are lots of things he can do well besides football." Calvin listened proudly as his brother was praised.

A boy in the Bible named David sang songs praising God. David's songs were prayers that said things like "your Name is near; people tell of your wonderful deeds" (Psalm 75:1). David cheered for God like Calvin cheered for his brother. Sometimes David's songs were prayers asking God for help.

You can praise God like David did. Some of God's names you can say in praise are holy God, King of kings, God of comfort, Lord of Lords, and God the creator. God's name is special. That's why we say his name is "hallowed," which means "greatly respected." For the next few days you'll be learning the Lord's Prayer!

Your Turn

1. How do you think God feels when you say words to praise him?

_____

_____

_____

Prayer

Father in heaven, I praise you because you are holy and good. Your names tell me how special you are. You are worth praising. Help me keep your name special and always in my heart. Amen.

How to Pray God's Way

Our Father in heaven, hallowed be your name...
– Matthew 6:9

God's Good Plans

Read this part of the Lord's Prayer out loud three times:

"Our Father in heaven, hallowed be your name" (Matthew 6:9).

Prayer

Help me to honor you name and respect it. Amen.

How to Pray God's Way

Our Father in heaven, hallowed be your name...
– Matthew 6:9

God's Good Provision

Say this part of the Lord's Prayer three times out loud.

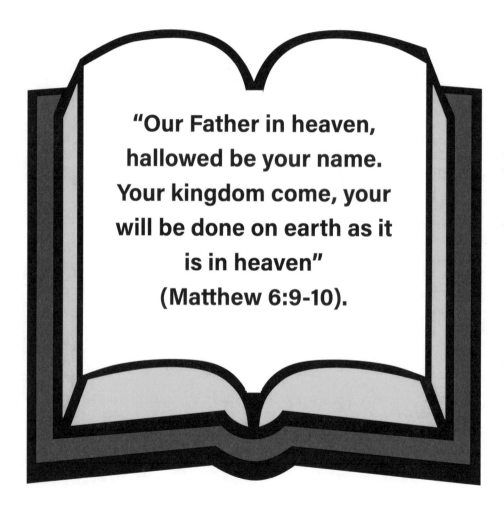

"Our Father in heaven,
hallowed be your name.
Your kingdom come, your
will be done on earth as it
is in heaven"
(Matthew 6:9-10).

Prayer

God, I want the things you approve of. Let your plans happen on earth as they do in heaven. Amen.

How to Pray God's Way

Our Father in heaven, hallowed be your name...
– Matthew 6:9

The Kingdom Dream

One night Tommy dreamed about God's heavenly kingdom. Three boys tried to get inside.

The first boy was Cory, who helped people. He was always helping his mother around the house. He even kept his room clean so his mother would have less work to do. Would Cory enter God's kingdom?

The second boy was Ben, who went around saying, "If the King loves his people, then everyone should be invited into his kingdom. The King would not turn anyone away." Would Ben make it into God's kingdom?

The third boy was Tanner. His family attended church. Tanner won a prize for learning 100 Bible verses. Would he be invited into God's kingdom?

Tommy woke up before any of the boys reached heaven's gates. What do you think happened to them?

How about you? To be invited into heaven is simple. You only have to believe Jesus died on the cross for your sins, ask him to forgive your sins, and choose to follow him.

Your Turn

1. Do you want to follow Jesus?
2. Have you asked him to be your Lord and Savior?

_____

_____

_____

Prayer

Lord Jesus, I believe in you. I know you died for me. Please forgive my sins. I will live for you from this moment on. Amen.

How to Pray God's Way

Our Father in heaven, hallowed be your name...
– Matthew 6:9

God's Care for you

Say this part of the Lord's Prayer out loud three times:

"Our Father in heaven, hallowed be your name. Your kingdom come, your will be done on earth as it is in heaven. Give us today our daily bread" (Matthew 6:9-11).

Prayer

God, thank you for making sure I have everything I need to follow you. I love you! Amen.

How to Pray God's Way

Our Father in heaven, hallowed be your name…
– Matthew 6:9

God's Forgiveness

Read this part of the Lord's Prayer out loud three times:

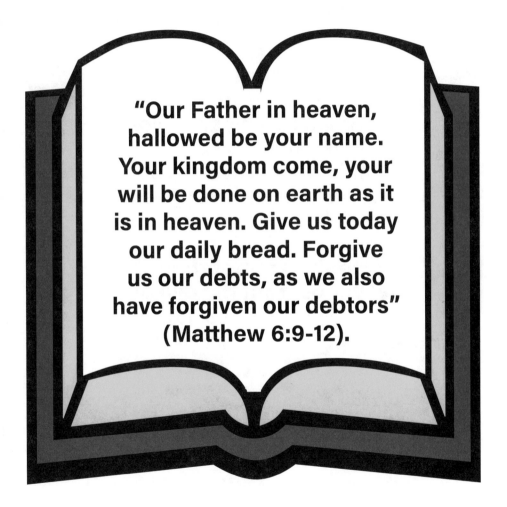

"Our Father in heaven, hallowed be your name. Your kingdom come, your will be done on earth as it is in heaven. Give us today our daily bread. Forgive us our debts, as we also have forgiven our debtors" (Matthew 6:9-12).

Prayer

God, I know I have done what I wanted, when I wanted. Please forgive me. Help me to be ready to forgive others just as you have forgiven me. Amen.

How to Pray God's Way

Our Father in heaven, hallowed be your name...
– Matthew 6:9

God's Perfect Prayer

Say the entire Lord's prayer three times out loud:

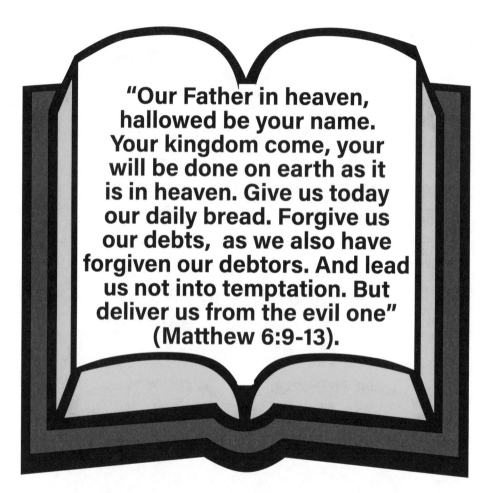

"Our Father in heaven, hallowed be your name. Your kingdom come, your will be done on earth as it is in heaven. Give us today our daily bread. Forgive us our debts, as we also have forgiven our debtors. And lead us not into temptation. But deliver us from the evil one" (Matthew 6:9-13).

**You did it! You can say the Lord's Prayer!
Use this prayer daily when you talk to God.**

Prayer

Dear Lord, thank you for giving me ways to stay away from temptation. I am excited that you have shown me how to pray. Amen.

Building God's Kingdom

The LORD will guide you always.
– Isaiah 58:11

God's Strong Crew

God's building crew includes his people;
    He helps each one conquer evil.
God gives good tools to help his crew:
    His Word and prayer, to name a few.
We ask God for his power and might
    To help us do his work just right.
We can trust him;
    He is the King;
He helps us in everything!

When you accept Jesus as your Lord and Savior, you are part of his building crew. He wants you to help people come to know him. God wants us to be a strong crew of mighty kids who serve and help him. Reading his Word and praying are important tools you have to grow strong in him.

The Bible is filled with stories of guys who used God's tools and worked on his building crew, including Jonah, Nehemiah, Joseph, Elijah, Joshua, Caleb, Joash, Philip, and Solomon.

Are you on God's building crew?

Your Turn

1. Why does God want you on his building crew?
2. What does God want you to help build?

_____

_____

_____

_____

Prayer

God, thank you for letting me be on your crew. Help me read your Word and pray. I want to help you make this world a better place. Amen.

Building God's Kingdom

The LORD will guide you always.
– Isaiah 58:11

Join God's Crew

Here are some of God's workers. Draw yourself in God's building crew.

Prayer

Lord, I want to be on your crew. Help me see people who need help and then show me how to help them. Amen.

Building God's Kingdom

The LORD will guide you always.
– Isaiah 58:11

You Can Do a Job for God

What job has God given you to do? Draw a picture of your job on the tool chest. Ask God to help you do a great job.

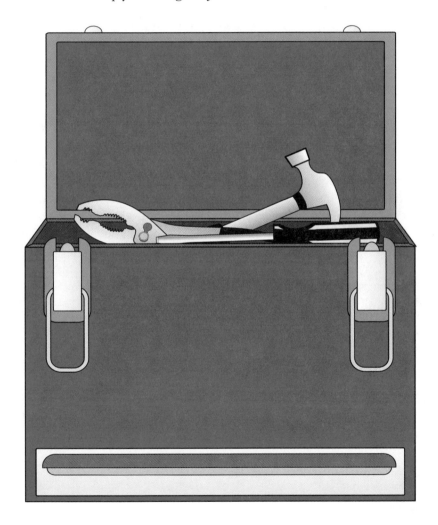

Prayer

God, I want to be a good worker for you. Help me do the best I can. Amen.

Building God's Kingdom

The LORD will guide you always.
– Isaiah 58:11

Neighborly Love

"I helped Mrs. Malone get her groceries into her house," Ryan told his mother.

"That's great!" Mom said. "She can use the help, since her husband died last month. It's good to help our neighbors."

"Mrs. Malone lives on the next street. She's not our neighbor."

Mom laughed. "'Neighbor' doesn't always mean someone right next door. A neighbor is anyone you meet. Do you remember the story Jesus told about neighbors?"

"No…" Ryan said.

"A man was traveling from one city to another. Along the way, bad people attacked him, took his clothes, and left him for dead. The first man who saw him walked on by. Another man came, and he crossed the street to avoid the injured man. A third man came by. He saw the hurt man lying in the road. His heart was filled with compassion. He bandaged the man's wounds. After putting him on his donkey, he took him to a hotel and paid for him to stay."

Mom paused. "Ryan, which of the three men do you think was a good neighbor to the hurt man?"

"The man who helped him," answered Ryan.

"Yes. And God wants us to do the same."

Your Turn

1. Write about a time you helped someone.

_____

_____

Prayer

Dear God, show me the neighbors you want me to help. Teach me to recognize when people are hurting. Amen.

Building God's Kingdom

The LORD will guide you always.
– Isaiah 58:11

God Has a Whale of a Job for You!

God had a job for Jonah, but Jonah did not want to do it. He got swallowed by a big fish when he didn't obey God. In the whale's mouth, write some jobs you can do for your family, friends, and neighbors. When you do one, put an "x" in the whale under the job.

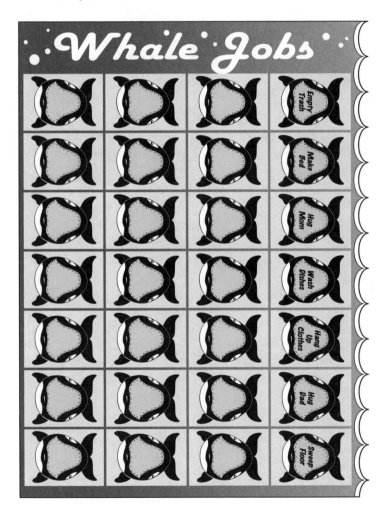

Prayer

God, I pray that people near and far from me will know your love. I pray that I will always obey you. Amen.

Building God's Kingdom

The LORD will guide you always.
– Isaiah 58:11

Who Are Your Neighbors?

On the mailboxes, write the names or draw pictures of your family members, friends, and neighbors you can help and love.

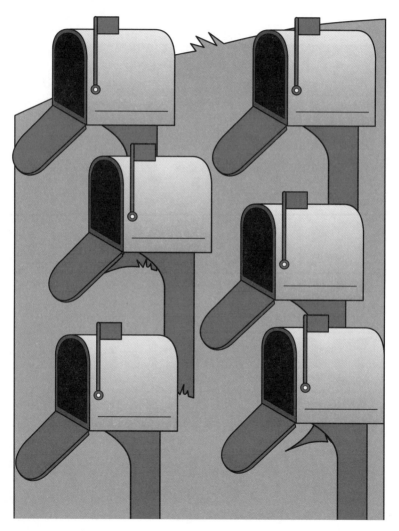

Prayer

God, your Word says to love my neighbors and help them. Show me the people you want me to help. Amen.

Building God's Kingdom

The LORD will guide you always.
– Isaiah 58:11

Two-Minute Listening

Practice listening. Sit quietly for two minutes and listen for sounds around your house. Write down or draw what you hear.

Prayer

Lord, help me to be quick to listen to your voice. Help me do what you want me to do for you. Amen.

Think About What Is Good

Whatever is true, whatever is noble, whatever is right, whatever is pure, whatever is lovely, whatever is admirable… think about such things.
– Philippians 4:8

Fix and Build

Kyle was so excited! The day before had been his birthday. His dad had given him a tool chest like his. The tools were smaller than Dad's, but they worked. "Now I can help Dad make things," Kyle said as he pulled out each tool and turned it over in his hand. Kyle loved to fix things that were broken.

The Bible tells of a man who also loved to fix things. Nehemiah worshipped and obeyed God. Nehemiah was sad because some enemies had broken down the city walls. So he prayed and asked God to help him. Then he went to look at the walls and made a plan to fix them. Nehemiah called a work crew together. The crew worked side-by-side to fix the walls.

What can you do to make your home better? God wants you to look for ways to improve things. You might not need a hammer and nails. God will help you stop fighting with your brothers and sisters, clean your room, and pick up your clothes.

Your Turn

1. What did Nehemiah fix?
2. What did Nehemiah do before making things better?

_____

_____

_____

_____

Prayer

God, help me see what I can do to make things better. I want to be like Nehemiah. I know you will help. Amen.

Think About What Is Good

Whatever is true, whatever is noble, whatever is right, whatever is pure, whatever is lovely, whatever is admirable… think about such things.
– Philippians 4:8

Your Gift List

Make a list of what you would like for Christmas or for your birthday. What is a way you could use some of theses things to help others or tell people about God.

Prayer

Lord, help me to think about things that are right, pure, and lovely to you. Amen.

Think About What Is Good

Whatever is true, whatever is noble, whatever is right, whatever is pure, whatever is lovely, whatever is admirable… think about such things.
– Philippians 4:8

What Should You Think?

Help the frog get through the maze as he changes from a mean, ugly frog to a nice, happy frog.

Prayer

God, help me to think on things that are good so I will be kind. I want to grow up thinking about Jesus and knowing him. Amen.

Think About What Is Good

Whatever is true, whatever is noble, whatever is right, whatever is pure, whatever is lovely, whatever is admirable... think about such things.
– Philippians 4:8

A Wish Wish

One day Mom asked her sons, "What would you like for your birthday?" Tony answered, "I want a bike, in-line skates, a scooter, and a video game."

Tommy said, "I'd like a plane ticket to go see Grandma. Since she is sick, I can take care of her. Also, I'd like a new Bible. I gave mine to a boy at school."

The boys were twins, but they were very different. Mom told Tony that he wouldn't get every item on his list. However, because Tommy had asked for things to help others, he would get all his requests.

Then Mom told Tony and Tommy about a wise man named Solomon. God said to King Solomon in a dream, "Ask for whatever you want me to give to you." King Solomon said, "Give your servant a discerning heart to govern your people and to distinguish right from wrong."

The Lord was pleased. "Since you have asked for this and not for long life or wealth for yourself...but for discernment in administering justice, I will do what you have asked. I will give you a wise and discerning heart...I will give you what you have not asked for—both wealth and honor" (1 Kings 3:11-13).

Your Turn

1. What would you ask God for?

_____

_____

_____

Prayer

Lord, thank you for helping me make good decisions. Help me be fair. Guide me so I will make right choices. Amen.

Think About What Is Good

Whatever is true, whatever is noble, whatever is right, whatever is pure, whatever is lovely, whatever is admirable... think about such things.
– Philippians 4:8

Make a Good Idea Happen

Here is an idea box. In the box, write or draw pictures of your ideas to serve God. Color the box and your drawings.

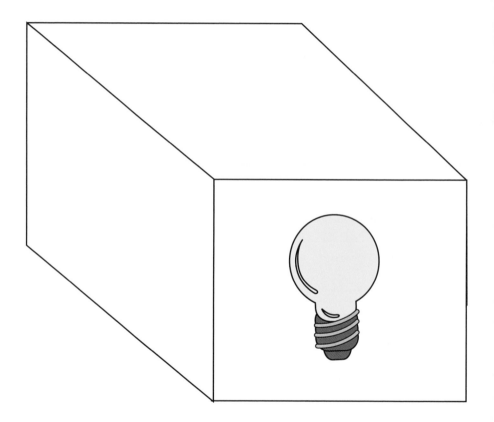

Prayer

Lord, show me how to serve you. Give me some good ideas I can use to do your work. I love you and want to help you any way I can. Amen.

Think About What Is Good

Whatever is true, whatever is noble, whatever is right, whatever is pure, whatever is lovely, whatever is admirable... think about such things.
– Philippians 4:8

God Has a Project for You

God told Noah to build a big ship called an ark. It took Noah and his sons many years to build it. Noah and his sons were willing to work hard. Finish building the ark for Noah. Notice the chores written on some of the ark's beams. Pick one of the chores and make that your project for today.

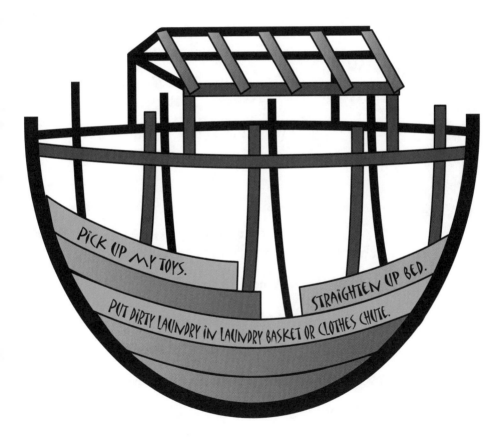

Prayer

Lord, show me how to serve you. Give me a project to do for you. Amen.

Think About What Is Good

Whatever is true, whatever is noble, whatever is right, whatever is pure, whatever is lovely, whatever is admirable… think about such things.
– Philippians 4:8

The Attitude Pledge

Read the pledge below and then say it out loud to God. Tell God you want him to build good attitudes in your life.

I pledge to build good attitudes in my life.

I will try to keep an attitude that is the same as Jesus's attitude.

I will show others that I need Jesus.

I will show Jesus that I'm sorry for my sin.

I will not act like I am better than others are.

I will always try to do the things that God's Word tells me I should do.

I will show kindness to others.

I will keep my heart clean from sin.

I will try to be a peacemaker wherever I go.

I will continue to do good things even if others treat me badly.

If people say bad things about me because I follow Jesus, I will be glad.

I know God will give me great happiness.

Prayer

God, help me follow you no matter what others say. Amen.

Jesus Stays Beside You

Come near to God and he will come near to you.
– James 4:8

The Rock Wall

Jack loved going to the gym with his dad. He had a blast climbing the 50-foot rock wall. Jack would feel strong at the start of his climb, but when he was halfway up his arms and legs would become weak. He couldn't get to the top.

One day, Jack's dad decided to climb the wall with him. As Jack climbed, his dad climbed beside him, talking to him with every step. "Up, up, up. Keep on climbing, son," Dad cheered.

"I can't go any farther," Jack told his dad as they reached the halfway point.

"Yes, you can, Jack," said Dad. "I'll climb beside you. Let's get to the top together."

Jack and his dad reached the top of the wall together. Jack was so happy! "I couldn't have made it to the top without you," Jack told his dad.

In some ways, Jesus is like Jack's father. Jesus is always willing to help you with the hard things. Whether it's taking a spelling test, working on a school project, or dealing with a bully, Jesus stays beside you.

Your Turn

1. How did Jack's dad help him reach the top?
2. How can Jesus help you?

_____

_____

_____

_____

Prayer

Jesus, I ask you to climb with me when things are hard. Thank you for staying beside me when things are difficult. Amen.

Jesus Stays Beside You

Come near to God and he will come near to you.
– James 4:8

Tornado Verses

Big storms can be scary. When you are afraid, remember that you can ask Jesus to calm your fears. Draw a picture or write in the center of this twister something that makes you afraid you afraid. Then look up the verses in the clouds.

Prayer

Dear Jesus, thank you for helping me when I am afraid. Teach me to trust in you when fear comes. Amen.

Jesus Stays Beside You

Come near to God and he will come near to you.
– James 4:8

My Climbing Wall

Let Jesus climb beside you when you want to accomplish something. No matter what is hard for you, Jesus will stay with you and encourage you. Draw yourself on the climbing wall. At the holds along the wall, write the things that are difficult for you to do.

Prayer

Jesus, even when life is hard I know I will make it because you are always with me. Thank you for never leaving my side. Amen.

Jesus Stays Beside You

Come near to God and he will come near to you.
– James 4:8

Little Cup

Once there was a little clay cup. The cup was very chipped and broken, so it was thrown into a place called the "Field of Broken Pots." The cup was thrown into a heap with other broken pieces of pottery.

One day, the master potter went walking through the field and found the little cup. The master potter was the one who had made it. He picked it up and carried it back to his house. The potter loved the little cup and wanted to remake it.

As the master potter put the little cup on the workbench, he whispered, "I love you, and I have a plan for you." The little cup didn't know it was about to be made like new. Its cracks, chips, and broken pieces would soon be repaired. The hand of the master potter would remake the cup.

Jesus is your Master Potter, and you are like the little cup. Your heart gets chipped and broken when your feelings are hurt. Things happen that make you feel sad and alone. When hard things happen, Jesus finds you and takes you under his care. When you say you're sorry, he forgives you. You are filled with joy again.

Your Turn

1. How is Jesus like a master potter?
2. How are you like the little cup?

_____

_____

_____

_____

Prayer

Dear Jesus, thank you for taking care of me. Thank you for taking me out of hurtful and scary places and making me like new. Amen.

Jesus Stays Beside You

Come near to God and he will come near to you.
– James 4:8

The Potter's House

Look at the items in the potter's house. Circle the things that you feel you need from Jesus right now.

Prayer

Dear Jesus, because you take care of me I am filled with joy. Thank you for taking my life and making it better. Amen.

Jesus Stays Beside You

Come near to God and he will come near to you.
– James 4:8

Helping Others

Sawhorses help people hold pieces of wood while they saw them into pieces for projects. How can you help people? Write your ideas under the sawhorse.

_____

_____

_____

_____

Prayer

Dear Jesus, please help me to love others and serve them. Amen.

Jesus Stays Beside You

Come near to God and he will come near to you.
– James 4:8

Jesus's Mercy

Use the code to solve the puzzle. Uncover what Jesus is willing to give you when you make mistakes.

d	e	g	n	p	o	a	v	m	c	r	n	y
1	2	3	4	5	6	7	8	9	10	11	12	13

_____
9   2   11   10   13

Prayer

Jesus, help me when I make a mistake. Show me how to do better next time. Amen.

God Enjoys You

Because of his great love for us,
God... made us alive with Christ.
– Ephesians 2:4-5

You Create Joy

"You were our little bundle of joy," Mom said as she pointed to Jimmy's baby pictures.

"I like being your joy!" he said. "But what does 'being your joy' mean?"

Mom smiled. "It means you make your dad and me smile and laugh. We love being with you. We enjoy you."

"Wow!" Jimmy said. "That makes me feel so important. Does God enjoy me too?"

"Yes, God enjoys you very much," answered Mom.

"But does he really, *really* enjoy me?" Jimmy asked.

"I'm telling you the truth, son," said Mom. "God really does enjoy you. He also enjoys your dad, your little brother, and me." She gave him a big hug. "The Bible tells us in Ephesians 1:4 that 'He chose us before the creation of the world to be holy and blameless in his sight.' So God loved you even before you were born!"

Jimmy smiled. "That makes my heart feel happy."

"God has been thinking of you for a very long time," said Mom. "You can count on always being enjoyed by him."

Your Turn

1. What are some things that you think God enjoys?

_____

_____

_____

Prayer

Dear God, you enjoy me more than I can know. Teach me your ways so I can enjoy you, too. Amen.

God Enjoys You

Because of his great love for us,
God... made us alive with Christ.
– Ephesians 2:4-5

My Enjoyment List

Make a list of the people in your life you like to spend time with. Write down the things about them you enjoy.

Prayer

Lord, I am so grateful that you love me and enjoy me. And I want to thank you for the people in my life I enjoy. Amen.

God Enjoys You

*Because of his great love for us,
God... made us alive with Christ.*
– Ephesians 2:4-5

Fill the Well with Love

On the well, list some ways that you can show love to others.

Prayer

Dear God, your love is like a bottomless well. Help me love others just as you love me. Amen.

God Enjoys You

Because of his great love for us,
God... made us alive with Christ.
– Ephesians 2:4-5

God Mends Broken Hearts

Chip was proud of the block tower he constructed. He grinned as he stood next to it. "This tower is as tall as me!" Hours of stacking blocks had paid off. Suddenly something soft brushed against Chip's leg and then...down went the blocks. Muffy, the family cat, had jumped on the tower.

"How will I rebuild my tower?" Chip wondered.

Like block towers, your heart can be broken because someone hurts you. Harmful teasing and unkind words can make your heart hurt. People might not mean to hurt you, but that's what happens. The good news is God wants to heal your hurts.

Jesus knows what it's like to have a broken heart. Many people rejected his teachings. They wanted to hurt him. One of his friends double-crossed him. But Jesus knew his Father would build him up again.

God wants to build your heart back up again. Tell him about your hurt feelings. Also, let your parents or your Sunday-school teacher help you. Holding hurt inside keeps your heart broken. Choose to receive God's love. Let him rebuild your heart with his love.

Your Turn

1. How can God help you deal with a broken heart?
2. Why should you share your feelings with your parents?

Prayer

Lord, I want to share my hurt with you. Show me your love and help heal the sad parts of my heart. Amen.

God Enjoys You

Because of his great love for us,
God... made us alive with Christ.
– Ephesians 2:4-5

The Rebuilt Heart

Draw a picture inside the broken heart that shows something that hurt your heart. Tell Jesus what you wish would happen. Receive his love and color the healed heart.

Prayer

Lord, I am so glad that I can share my hurt feelings with you, and that you will help to heal my hurting heart. Amen.

God Enjoys You

Because of his great love for us,
God… made us alive with Christ.
– Ephesians 2:4-5

Family Portrait

Draw the members of your family in the picture frame. Then say a prayer thanking God for each one of them.

Prayer

Dear Lord, I love my family. Help me to tell and show them that I love them. Amen.

God Enjoys You

Because of his great love for us,
God... made us alive with Christ.
– Ephesians 2:4-5

Words of Love

On this list write the names of some people you love. Now write a sentence for each one that says one thing about them that you especially like. This week tell them what you wrote.

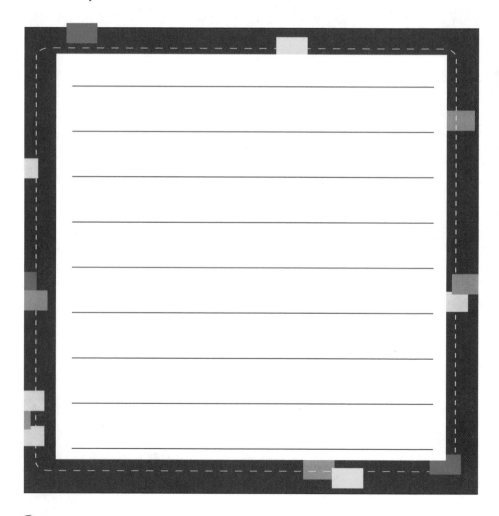

Prayer

God, when I am kind to others, my heart is happy. Help me remember to be kind to people and say nice things to them often. Amen.

God Loves Compassionate Hearts

Be kind and compassionate to one another,
forgiving each other, just as in Christ God forgave you.
– Ephesians 4:32

Forgiving Is Obeying God

The disciple Peter came to Jesus with a question. "How many times shall I forgive my brother or sister who sins against me? Up to seven times?"

Jesus answered, "Not seven times, but seventy times seven" (Matthew 18:21-22).

That's a lot of times! Jesus wanted Peter—and you—to know that it is important to have a forgiving heart. It doesn't matter how often somebody does something bad to you. Forgiving is obeying God.

Forgiving means you stop carrying the hurt in your heart. You don't think about getting back at the person who hurt you. Forgiveness is like erasing chalk marks on a chalkboard. Jesus will help you.

Just because the hurt is forgiven doesn't mean it didn't happen. It just means you choose not to let your heart be marked up by the hurt anymore.

Do you have bad feelings in your heart? Ask Jesus to help you choose to forgive. Make forgiveness and obedience to Jesus your goals.

Your Turn

1. What was Peter asking Jesus?
2. What does it mean to forgive?

_____

_____

_____

_____

Prayer

Dear God, show me anyone I need to forgive. Help me know I need to let you handle the hurts in my life. Amen.

God Loves Compassionate Hearts

Be kind and compassionate to one another,
forgiving each other, just as in Christ God forgave you.
– Ephesians 4:32

Jesus Said to Forgive

Draw seventy-seven crosses on the Bible cover. That's a lot of crosses! God wants us to forgive over and over again.

Prayer

Dear Lord, I know you want me to forgive others, but sometimes that is hard. I want to forgive because I know that will please you. Pleasing you makes me happy. Amen.

God Loves Compassionate Hearts

*Be kind and compassionate to one another,
forgiving each other, just as in Christ God forgave you.*
– Ephesians 4:32

Heart Darts

Write the name of a person you need to forgive near the dart on the dartboard. Then ask God to help you to forgive him or her.

_____

Prayer

Dear God, I know that with your help I can forgive whoever has hurt me. Thank you for your help. Amen.

God Loves Compassionate Hearts

Be kind and compassionate to one another,
forgiving each other, just as in Christ God forgave you.
– Ephesians 4:32

Is Your Heart Happy?

Is your heart a happy heart? God wants you to enjoy the life he's given you. It's hard to smile on the outside when you are sad on the inside. Long-lasting problems can make you sad. David's heart was happy. "The LORD has done great things for us, and we are filled with joy" (Psalm 126:3). How do you get a happy heart?

When you know God loves you, you are glad inside. Part of knowing God is talking to him. Sharing your feelings with your loving heavenly Father will help you keep your heart happy. You can tell Him everything. Build a happy heart in this way:

> First, tell God about a problem you have and how you feel.
> Second, share every secret with him.
> Third, choose to forgive any people involved in your problem.
> Fourth, let go of anger and hurt, like shooting an arrow.
> Fifth, give your thoughts about the problem to Jesus.
> Sixth, thank God for loving you and caring for you.

David also wrote, "I cry aloud to the LORD...I tell him my trouble" (Psalm 142:1-2). Telling God how you feel helps build a happy heart.

Your Turn

1. How can it help to tell God your problems?

_____

_____

_____

Prayer

Dear Lord, give me the courage to share my feelings. Amen.

God Loves Compassionate Hearts

Be kind and compassionate to one another,
forgiving each other, just as in Christ God forgave you.
– Ephesians 4:32

The Happy Heart

Draw a happy face in the heart to show God wants you to be happy. Color the heart.

Prayer

Lord, I know you want me to have a happy heart. Remind me to pray every day and ask you to help me. Amen.

God Loves Compassionate Hearts

Be kind and compassionate to one another,
forgiving each other, just as in Christ God forgave you.
– Ephesians 4:32

Jesus Paid the Price

Jesus paid a price to buy you back for God. Create a special dollar bill by drawing Jesus's face in the center.

Prayer

Dear Jesus, thank you for paying to get me back for God. You are amazing! Amen.

God Loves Compassionate Hearts

Be kind and compassionate to one another,
forgiving each other, just as in Christ God forgave you.
– Ephesians 4:32

A Text Message to God

Part of knowing God is talking to him. Sharing your feelings with your Father in heaven will help you keep your heart happy. Text God, thanking him for loving you and letting you talk to him about everything.

Prayer

Thank you, God, that I can share everything with you. Help me let go of any anger, hurt, and unforgiveness. I know you will take care of it. Amen.

God Loves Strong Hearts

*Walk in the way of love, just as Christ loved us
and gave himself up for us.*
– Ephesians 5:2

The Best Player

Mr. Payne heard children's voices in the yard.

"I'm the best!"

"No, I'm the best!"

Mr. Payne decided he should talk with the kids. He took some cookies and juice outside, and as the kids snacked, he told them a Bible story. He said, "One day Jesus's helpers started arguing. Each of them thought he should be the leader.

"When Jesus heard this, he said, 'Anyone who wants to be first must be the very last, and the servant of all.' That means if you want to be great for God, you must help others. Jesus also said, 'The Son of Man did not come to be served, but to serve.'"

Mr. Payne finished and waited as the kids thought about the Bible story. They felt bad about their arguing. They realized that if somebody wants to be great, he needs to encourage others. They were wrong to argue about who was the best. That didn't matter.

Great people are those willing to be last. Jesus was always thinking about God and putting people before himself. He always helped people.

Your Turn

1. Why do you think Jesus was so great?

_____

_____

_____

_____

Prayer

Dear Lord, forgive me when I try to be more important than others. Teach me to put others ahead of me. Amen.

God Loves Strong Hearts

Walk in the way of love, just as Christ loved us
and gave himself up for us.
– Ephesians 5:2

The Last Boy

Here's a football team. Draw your face on the faceless boy in the back of the huddle. Show God you're willing to be last and to serve others. Remember: Great people are those willing to put others first.

Prayer

Dear God, I want to be great in your eyes. Help me to have a strong heart for you and choose to help others. Amen.

God Loves Strong Hearts

*Walk in the way of love, just as Christ loved us
and gave himself up for us.*
– Ephesians 5:2

A Calculator

Who can help you solve your problems? Use the code to punch the buttons on the calculator to find name of the very best problem solver!

KEY

1 2 3 4 5 6 7 8 9
A J W E S O R U L

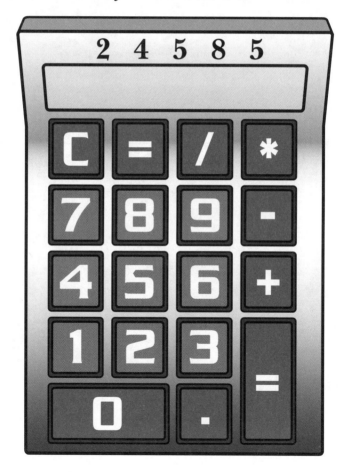

Prayer

Dear Lord, help me give my problems to you. You are the ultimate problem solver. Amen.

God Loves Strong Hearts

*Walk in the way of love, just as Christ loved us
and gave himself up for us.*
– Ephesians 5:2

Think of Others

A ship wrecked in a storm. Two boys, Ryan and Brady, were able to swim to a small island. Once there, they agreed to pray. They wanted to see whose prayers got results, so they divided the island into two parts. Each boy stayed on his side of the island and prayed for help.

Ryan prayed for food. The next morning, he saw a fruit tree on his side. He ate all the fruit, so Brady went hungry.

Ryan prayed for shelter, clothes, and food. The next day, all those things appeared. Ryan didn't share even though Brady still had nothing.

Finally, Ryan prayed for a ship to come so he could leave the island. The next morning, a ship came and Ryan boarded it, leaving Brady behind.

Brady doesn't deserve God's blessings because his prayers weren't answered, Ryan thought. Then he heard God's voice.

"Why are you leaving Brady behind?"

"I was the one whose prayers were answered," replied Ryan. "I'm the one worthy of leaving."

"You're wrong," God told him. "Brady prayed only one prayer, which I answered."

"What did he pray?" Ryan asked.

"He prayed for your prayers to be answered."

Your Turn

1. Why was God not pleased with Ryan?

2. Why was God pleased with Brady?

Prayer

Dear God, keep me from selfishness and an ungrateful heart. I want to have an unselfish heart toward my family and friends. Amen.

God Loves Strong Hearts

*Walk in the way of love, just as Christ loved us
and gave himself up for us.*
– Ephesians 5:2

The Key

Jesus is the key to a happy heart. Will you let him be your locksmith and give you a happy heart?

Trace the key on the heart below. Now write your name on the heart and color the key.

Prayer

Dear Lord, show me where my heart is locked. Help me open my heart to you. I want to give my whole heart to you. Amen.

God Loves Strong Hearts

Walk in the way of love, just as Christ loved us
and gave himself up for us.
– Ephesians 5:2

Give It Away

The Bible says that God loves a cheerful giver. Can you think of something God wants you to give to someone? Draw a picture of it.

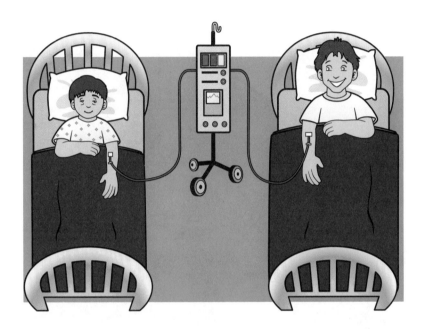

Prayer

God, teach me to be a true giver. Thank you for giving so much to me. Amen.

God Loves Strong Hearts

*Walk in the way of love, just as Christ loved us
and gave himself up for us.*
– Ephesians 5:2

Selfish or Unselfish Island?

Do you remember the story of the two shipwrecked boys? Look at the two sides of the island. According to the story, which side of the island do you think God wants you to be on? Draw yourself on that side.

Prayer

Dear God, help me be loving and kind to my friends and family. If I can help them, show me how to help. Amen.

God Wants to Clean Your Heart

Create in me a clean heart, O God.
– Psalm 51:10 KJV

The Opposites

As Avery came out of the bathroom, his dad asked, "Did you wash your hands?"

Avery nodded.

But when Dad saw his son's hands he said, "You forgot to use soap. Check the backs of your hands and your fingers. See the dirt? Go back and wash up."

The second time, Avery got his hands very clean.

Like Avery, you can clean yourself on the outside. Only God can wash you on the inside. Forcing yourself to be good on the outside does not change your insides. God is more concerned about how clean your insides—your heart and your mind—are.

Have you ever seen a white shirt or towel with black spots on it? It's the first thing people notice. In the same way, dark spots on your heart can be seen by your friends and family by how you act. When your heart has a bad attitude, your outside behavior usually is that way too.

Jesus died on the cross so your heart can be made clean again. The Bible says that he is the light of the world. When he comes into your life, his light fills the dark places of your heart.

Your Turn

1. What can Jesus wash clean in your life?
2. What do you need to do to get a clean heart?

_____

_____

_____

Prayer

Jesus, I want you as my Savior. Make my heart clean. Change the dark in my heart to your light. Amen.

God Wants to Clean Your Heart

Create in me a clean heart, O God.
– Psalm 51:10 KJV

Cross It Out

Mark out the spots on the heart with a cross over each one. The cross will remind you that Jesus died on the cross to take away your sins.

Prayer

Dear Jesus, thank you that by willingly dying on the cross for me you took away my sins. I am so thankful that You are my Lord and Savior. Amen.

God Wants to Clean Your Heart

Create in me a clean heart, O God.
– Psalm 51:10 KJV

The Car Wash

This car is dirty! Wash away the sins by coloring over them. Below the car write this week's verse to help you remember it.

_____

_____

_____

Prayer

Dear God, please help me keep my heart clean. When I don't keep my heart clean, remind me to ask for your forgiveness so you will wash away my sins. Amen.

God Wants to Clean Your Heart

Create in me a clean heart, O God.
– Psalm 51:10 KJV

White as Snow

White is usually considered clean. It is the color of fluffy clouds in the sky, a new baseball, and snow. It also reflects the heart of someone who knows Jesus.

Jeffrey asked his mother, "Where do our sins go after God forgives them?"

Mom smiled. "Remember when you helped Dad wash and wax the car?" she asked. "It was covered with tar, dirt, and other dark spots. Where do you think the marks on the cars went?"

"I don't know," Jeffrey answered. "Daddy told me we were rubbing away the marks."

"That's right," said Mom. "You and Dad wiped them all away. They aren't on the car any longer, and they're all gone. That's what happens to our sins when God forgives them."

Jesus wants to wipe away your sins. No matter what bad thing you do, including lying or being selfish, Jesus is ready to take away your sin. All you have to do is ask him for forgiveness, accept his cleaning, and try not to sin again. Jesus will make your heart as white as snow.

Your Turn

1. What should you do if you've done something wrong?
2. What happens to your sins when they are forgiven?

_____

_____

_____

Prayer

Dear God, wash away my sin. I'm sorry for doing what I want and not what you want. Teach me to do things your way. Amen.

God Wants to Clean Your Heart

Create in me a clean heart, O God.
– Psalm 51:10 KJV

A Clean Heart

Color all the spaces that have the letter H, E, A, R, and T. Then count how many times you see the words "CLEAN" and "HEART" in the puzzle. (If you want, you can also use a different color for the spaces that have the letters C, L, E, A, and N.)

Prayer

Dear Jesus, I am so glad you have made a way for me to get a clean heart. Teach me to live the way you want me to. Amen.

God Wants to Clean Your Heart

Create in me a clean heart, O God.
– Psalm 51:10 KJV

Pathway to the Cross

At the top of the maze, draw a picture of you. Find the path that gets you to the cross. You can use a crayon, marker, or your finger to trace the path. The cross reminds you that Jesus will make your heart clean.

Prayer

Dear Jesus, I am so happy that I know you as my Lord and Savior. Because you carried my sins to the cross, I am saved. Thank you! Amen.

God Wants to Clean Your Heart

Create in me a clean heart, O God.
– Psalm 51:10 KJV

Live in the Light

Think of your favorite shirt. What would it look like if you fell down in a mud puddle? That shirt is like your heart. When you choose to do things that are bad, your heart gets dirty. You can be happy about your heart because Jesus will make it clean again! All you have to do is say you are sorry and ask for forgiveness.

Draw two hearts in the box. Color one so it looks like it was in a mud puddle. Write "Jesus" on the second, clean heart. He is the only One who can make your heart clean and like new again.

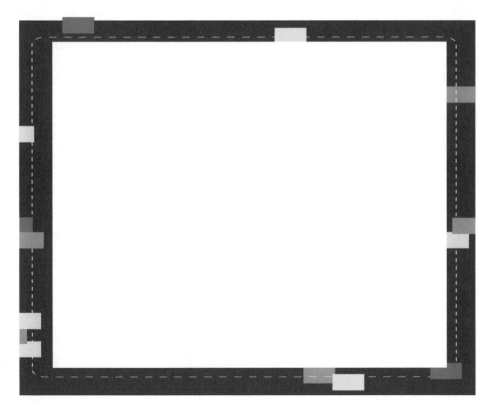

Prayer

Dear Jesus, I want to live in your light where my heart is clean. Help me to choose your will for my life. Amen.

Believe with All Your Heart

I know whom I have believed, and am convinced that he is able.
– 2 Timothy 1:12

Why Do You Believe?

There have always been people who don't believe in God. In fact, God sent Jesus to show people how to live. Jesus walked on water and did all kinds of miracles to try to teach people about God. But some people didn't believe he was God's Son, so they killed him.

Jesus was good and kind like his Father in heaven. He told God that the people didn't know what they were doing when they killed him. Jesus asked his father to forgive them. Jesus died, but he rose from his grave and is now back in heaven with God.

Jesus helps his Father in heaven by listening to your prayers. You can pray any time you want, and Jesus and God are sure to hear you. That's because they are on duty at all times.

If you believe in God, you are never alone. Your parents and your friends cannot always be with you, but God can. He goes with you to school, to camp, to church, and to the park. He is with you when you are afraid of the dark. He helps you when you have a spelling test.

But you shouldn't just think about what God can do for you. You should think of who God is. He is kind, helpful, and caring. He comes into your life and loves you. He made you and cares for you. Believe in him.

Your Turn

1. Do you believe in God and Jesus? Why or why not?
2. How can you find out more about God and Jesus?

_____

_____

_____

Prayer

Dear God, I want to believe in you more and more each day. Show yourself to me. I believe in you with all my heart. Amen.

Believe with All Your Heart

I know whom I have believed, and am convinced that he is able.
– 2 Timothy 1:12

My Earth Poster

On the earth, draw a picture of something you need to ask forgiveness for. Ask God to forgive you. He will forgive you. He will send your sin as far as the east is from the west.

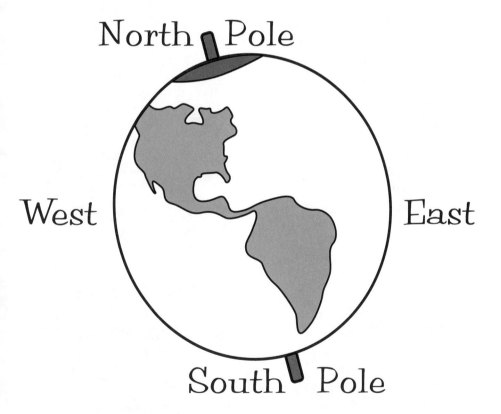

Prayer

Dear Lord, thank you for forgiving my sins. Amen.

Believe with All Your Heart

I know whom I have believed, and am convinced that he is able.
– 2 Timothy 1:12

Don't Sit on the Fence

God is able to give you the strength and courage to do the right thing. The boy is climbing the fence. Which side of the fence do you think God wants him on? Draw him on that side.

Prayer

Dear Jesus, with your help I have the courage to do the right thing. I am strong with you. Amen.

Believe with All Your Heart

I know whom I have believed, and am convinced that he is able.
– 2 Timothy 1:12

Elevators

Preston liked to go to the mall with his mother. He enjoyed pushing the elevator buttons, but mostly he loved riding up and down. His stomach felt a tickle when the elevator took him to the next floor. The doors opened to reveal a surprise. He loved seeing new faces when the doors slid open. "I like to ride the elevator," Preston told his mother.

"I like it too!" said Mom. "Elevators take us to the top floor so we don't need to climb stairs."

Jesus is kind of like an elevator. Elevators are the way to get to the top floor of a building. Jesus is the way to get to heaven. People who know Jesus, who love and trust him, will go to heaven.

Long ago, one of Jesus's friends, a disciple named Thomas, asked, "How can we know the way [to heaven]?"

Jesus said, "I am the way and the truth and the life" (John 14:6).

Jesus doesn't just tell us how to get to heaven. He is the way to heaven! Knowing him will take you there.

Isn't it wonderful to know you can be in heaven with God and Jesus someday? When you love and serve God now, you are preparing to see him later in heaven. Also, knowing and loving God makes your life on earth better. God wants you to know him!

Your Turn

1. In what way is Jesus like the elevator?

_____

_____

_____

Prayer

Dear Jesus, I am glad you are the only way to heaven. I know I can't get to heaven without knowing you. I want you to be my God. Amen.

Believe with All Your Heart

I know whom I have believed, and am convinced that he is able.
– 2 Timothy 1:12

An Elevator Prayer

Use the clues for each floor on the elevator to write a prayer to God. Read the prayer to him when you are finished.

Thank You, God, for sending (1) _____ to die on the

(2)_____ for me. I know my (3) _____ are (8)_____.

I want to (4) _____ Your (7)_____ and

(5)_____ You. Thank You for (6)_____ (9)_____.

Thank You that some day I can live with You in (10)_____.

Prayer

Dear Jesus, I want to know you more. I'm glad I'm going to live forever in heaven with you. Thank you. Amen.

Believe with All Your Heart

I know whom I have believed, and am convinced that he is able.
– 2 Timothy 1:12

Run to God

There's a storm brewing! God will help you not be afraid. Find the path that leads to safety. Use a pencil, or marker, or trace the path with your finger.

Prayer

Dear Lord, I believe you will help me in all circumstances. When I need help, I will pray and ask for Your comfort. Amen.

Believe with All your Heart

I know whom I have believed, and am convinced that he is able.
– 2 Timothy 1:12

Empty your Pack

Write your sins on the boy's backpack. Now write the same words on Jesus's backpack. Color your pack with a dark color so the words you wrote can't be seen. Let Jesus take away your sins. That's how you have a clean heart when you go to heaven.

Prayer

Jesus, thank you for loving me and getting rid of my sins. I want to be with you now and in heaven.

God's Free Gift

The gift of God is eternal life in Christ Jesus.
– Romans 6:23

Grandma's Gift

Tony's grandma brought a gift to his birthday party, but Tony didn't open it right away. Instead, he put it with the other gifts. Tony was having too much fun at his party to open Grandma's gift. He knew it would take time to open the gift, and he might want to play with it. Plus, he would need to thank Grandma and talk with her about the gift. So he chose to wait.

God offers everyone a free gift—forgiveness of sins. But many people don't fully accept God's gift. They take it and put it aside. Perhaps they believe they are too busy thinking to pay attention to God.

Yet when something goes wrong, these people turn to God to get them out of their messes. That's like having a gift but opening it only when absolutely necessary out of fear instead of gratitude.

Receive God's gift and open it right away. When you fully accept God's gift of salvation, you let him be in charge of your life. He will help you be happy.

After Tony's friends left his party, he finally opened Grandma's gift. He really liked it and wished he had opened it sooner. God's gift is the best gift you will ever receive. Open it now!

Your Turn

1. Have you accepted God's gift?
2. What can you tell your friends about God's wonderful gift?

_____

_____

_____

Prayer

Dear Jesus, thank you for your free gift of salvation. I want to accept it fully and live your way. Amen.

God's Free Gift

The gift of God is eternal life in Christ Jesus.
– Romans 6:23

My Salvation Verse Bank

Knowing where the Scripture verses about God's great gift will help you stay on his path. Keeping some of the verses together in this bank will help. Color your bank and look up the verses. Copy the bank and put it where you will see it often. As you learn more verses, add them to the bank.

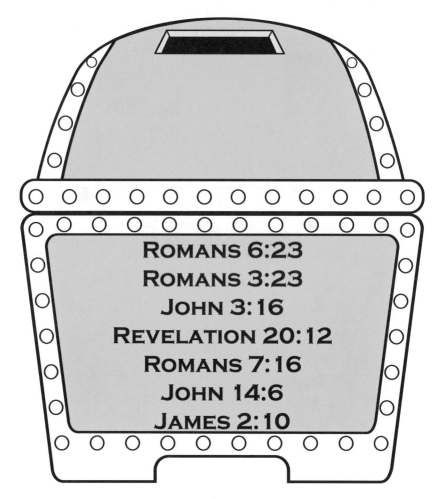

ROMANS 6:23
ROMANS 3:23
JOHN 3:16
REVELATION 20:12
ROMANS 7:16
JOHN 14:6
JAMES 2:10

Prayer

Dear Jesus, thank you for your plan of salvation. I want to tell people about you so they can be saved, too. Amen.

God's Free Gift

The gift of God is eternal life in Christ Jesus.
– Romans 6:23

A Gift Bag

Are there things keeping you from accepting God's free gift of salvation? Write your thoughts in the center of the bag. Decorate the rest of the free gift bag with crayons or markers.

Prayer

Dear Jesus, if there is anything that is keeping me from fully accepting your free gift of salvation, please help me to see it and give it to you. I want you to be the most important thing in my life. Amen.

God's Free Gift

The gift of God is eternal life in Christ Jesus.
– Romans 6:23

Aunt Hattie's Hugs

Travis and Tyler rode their bikes to their Great-Aunt Hattie's house. Aunt Hattie always had cookies waiting for them at the kitchen table.

"I'm helping out at the Salvation Army later today," Aunt Hattie told the boys as they munched their cookies.

"What is sal-wa-tion?" Tyler asked, sounding out the word.

"And what's it got to do with an army?" Travis asked.

Aunt Hattie laughed. "The Salvation Army is not a real army. It is a ministry that helps poor people."

"I think my Sunday-school teacher says that sal-wa-tion word," Tyler said. "But I don't know what it means."

"It is not sal-wa-tion, it is sal-va-tion," Aunt Hattie corrected with a smile. "Salvation means that Jesus saved us so we can know him now and live with him in heaven someday." She opened her Bible. "John 3:16 says, 'God so loved the world that he gave his one and only Son.' "

Travis pointed to some words. "Look! It says that if we believe in Jesus, we will live forever."

"Right!" said Aunt Hattie. "That's what salvation means. Jesus saved us from our sins. When we believe in him, we do what he wants." Aunt Hattie's eyes twinkled as she talked with the boys about Jesus. He was one of her favorite subjects!

Your Turn

1. What does "salvation" mean?
2. Have you accepted Jesus's gift of salvation?

_____

_____

_____

Prayer

Dear Jesus, thank you for salvation. I love you. Amen.

God's Free Gift

The gift of God is eternal life in Christ Jesus.
– Romans 6:23

Grateful News Flash

Show Jesus you are grateful that he died for you. Write your own blog on the computer screen. Tell Jesus you are grateful that he has saved you from your sins.

Prayer

Dear Jesus, thank you for dying for my sins. Thank you, God, for sending Jesus to die for me. Thank you for forgiving my sins. Amen.

God's Free Gift

The gift of God is eternal life in Christ Jesus.
– Romans 6:23

The Beautiful Cross

Let this cross remind you that Jesus died for you. Decorate the cross as a way to remember that Jesus took your sins away and gave you salvation.

Prayer

Dear Jesus, thank you for dying in my place. Thank you for taking the hurt for my wrong actions. Amen.

God's Free Gift

The gift of God is eternal life in Christ Jesus.
– Romans 6:23

Trading Places Word Scramble

Who was willing to die for you? Unscramble the letters below to find out.

U E S J S

_____

Prayer

Dear Jesus, thank you for coming into my life and being my Lord and Savior.
Amen.

Build Your Life Right

Have the same mindset as Christ Jesus.
– Philippians 2:5

Inside and Outside

"Should I use my inside or outside voice?" Ryan asked his mother as they walked through a downtown courtyard that had a roof but no walls.

Mom laughed. "That's a good question. We are kind of inside and outside, aren't we?"

Like the courtyard, did you know that you have an inside and an outside life? Outside is the part of you that everyone sees. It's what you look like, what you do, what you like to eat, and the people you choose to hang around with.

Your inside life contains the hidden things no one can see unless you tell them. It's your feelings, fears, likes, dislikes, and the things you don't talk about. Your inside feelings include how you look at the world, and that comes out in your attitude.

Sometimes when you are asked to obey God, your inside feelings don't want to. So you might disobey with a mad look on your face. That is called a bad attitude. God wants your inside attitude to be the same as Jesus's attitude. Jesus was willing to obey his Father in heaven with a happy heart. He wants you to have a good attitude so your outside will shine brightly for him.

Your Turn

1. What is the attitude Jesus had?
2. How can Jesus help you build a good attitude?

_____

_____

_____

Prayer

God, I praise you because you gave me the ability to feel and think. You never stop thinking about me—that's how much you love me. Help me to have a good attitude toward obeying you and my parents. Amen.

Build your Life Right

Have the same mindset as Christ Jesus.
– Philippians 2:5

Outside–Inside Sack

Pretend this sack is you. Decorate the outside with your favorite colors. On the inside part of the sack, write a short prayer asking Jesus to help you have a good attitude.

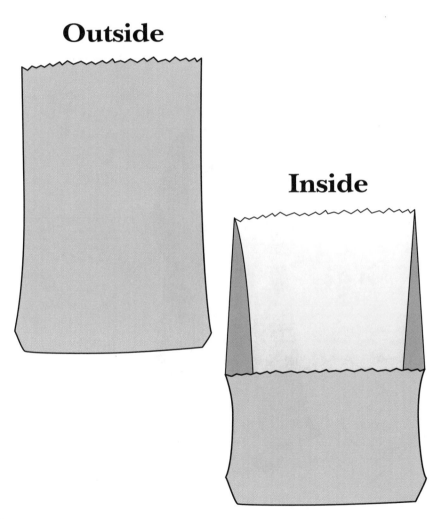

Outside

Inside

Prayer

Jesus, I want to have the same attitude you have. Please give me the desire to love and help people. Amen.

Build Your Life Right

Have the same mindset as Christ Jesus.
– Philippians 2:5

A King's Heart

King David was a man with strong muscles and a soft heart. The Bible says David was a man after God's own heart. Color the hearts that show a heart like King David had.

Prayer

Dear God, make me a guy with a soft heart. I want to have a heart like King David. Let me have a humble heart that is tender toward you. Amen.

Build Your Life Right

Have the same mindset as Christ Jesus.
– Philippians 2:5

Depend on God

"Who does God depend on for help?" Brandon asked his dad one day.

"God doesn't depend on anyone for help," Dad answered. "He can do anything. He is all-powerful. He made heaven and earth. If he needs something, He can create it just by speaking it."

Brandon said, "Wow! God can always help us."

"Yes," said Dad, "He wants us to depend on him. Jesus said, 'Blessed are the poor in spirit, for theirs is the kingdom of heaven.' That means God never expects us to make it on our own in life. We have him."

"I get it. He wants us to turn to him," said Brandon. "Like when I need to know my math facts. God wants me to ask him to help me focus when I study. Maybe God can help me do my best in sports?"

"God can do anything," said Dad. "Now let's go practice your batting."

Brandon got it right. When you think you can do everything on your own, you aren't following God's way. Some kids brag, saying they can run, hop, skip, and jump better than anyone else. They depend on themselves to do well. That is not God's way.

Jesus teaches that being kind to others pleases God. You do not need to brag to feel important. You are important because you are God's child. Be the best you can be for God by depending on him.

Your Turn

1. What can you do when you remember that you need God?

2. If someone says he is better than you, what can you say?

_____

_____

_____

Prayer

Dear Jesus, show me how to be who you want me to be. Amen.

Build Your Life Right

Have the same mindset as Christ Jesus.
– Philippians 2:5

Needy Nail Trail

Follow the trail of nails with a crayon or marker to see Who wants to meet your needs. Fill in the blanks along the trail with things you need to rely on God for. For example, you might write, "I need God's help in math."

Prayer

God, I need your help, and I know that when I pray you will answer. Thank you. Amen.

Build Your Life Right

Have the same mindset as Christ Jesus.
– Philippians 2:5

Sorry Scissors

Use the scissors to cut wrong behavior and attitudes from your life. Write below the blades something you need to say you are sorry for. Then ask for God's forgiveness and help. If you need to, tell the person involved you are sorry too.

_____

_____

_____

_____

Prayer

Dear God, sometimes I do things I shouldn't do. Teach me to be sorry for those things and remind me to apologize to anyone I have hurt. Amen.

Build Your Life Right

Have the same mindset as Christ Jesus.
– Philippians 2:5

Building Your Life Right

Draw a building around these words that will help you live the way God wants you to.

Respect

Kindness

Obedience

Honesty

Truthfulness

Prayer

Dear God, help me to want to do right. Help me build my life with your love. Amen.

Set Your Mind on God

My thoughts are not your thoughts, neither are your ways my ways.
– Isaiah 55:8

God's Thinking Is Better

Chris loved playing baseball. He always did his best for the team. Sadly, he didn't get along well with one of his coaches. Chris felt as if he could never do anything right for Coach Simon. Chris decided to quit. When Chris talked with his parents, they told him not to quit. They said he should pray instead. He should ask God to change the situation.

Chris couldn't understand why God would want him to keep playing with such a mean coach. "How could God possibly think the way I'm being treated is right?" he asked his parents.

"God doesn't think the way we think," Dad told him. "You see, God wants you to learn to trust him to help you and not quit when things are hard. God does not always do what we want, but his ways are always best for us. You'll see."

So Chris went back to practice and started praying for Coach Simon.

At the end of the season, Coach Simon pulled Chris aside. "Chris, I know you think I'm harder on you than the other kids. That's because I think you show real talent. As a matter of fact, I'd like to continue working with you on your pitching during the off- season. I think by next summer you'll be ready to play with the older kids."

"Wow!" Chris thought. "I'm glad I stayed on the team. God is cool!"

Your Turn

1. What was God's plan for Chris?
2. What do you need to ask God to help you with?

Prayer

Dear God, help me trust you. I'm glad you think differently than I do. You always look out for me. Amen.

Set Your Mind on God

My thoughts are not your thoughts, neither are your ways my ways.
– Isaiah 55:8

Cheerful Thoughts Box

Jesus came to show people how to have cheerful minds. He wanted people to know they could trust God no matter what. Jesus will help you be cheerful too. In the box, write down words that will remind you of the good things God wants you to think about and do that will help you be happy.

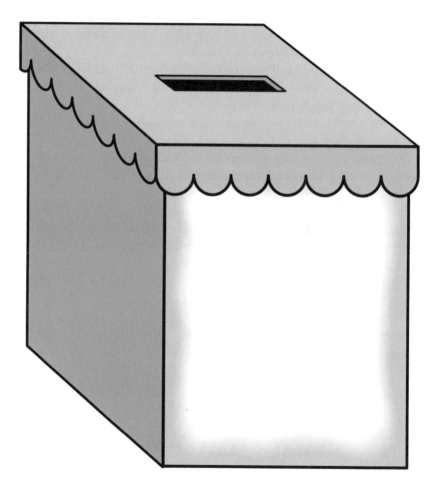

Prayer

Dear God, please help me have a cheerful mind. Teach me to change my bad thinking habits. I want to be thankful about everything. Amen.

Set Your Mind on God

My thoughts are not your thoughts, neither are your ways my ways.
– Isaiah 55:8

Mind Battles

Do you sometimes have bad thoughts? Reading the Bible can help you fight those bad thoughts. Look at the battlefield. Draw an X over the warriors who have bad attitudes. Write down good attitudes for the other warriors.

Jealousy

Lies

Doubt

Mistrust

Prayer

God, I want to change my thinking. Help me learn your Word so I can develop a mind like yours. I want to think like you do. Amen.

Set Your Mind on God

My thoughts are not your thoughts, neither are your ways my ways.
– Isaiah 55:8

Prepare Your Mind

A "willing" mind is eager to please God by listening and obeying him. When you go somewhere, you prepare for the trip. You pack your clothes, turn off the lights, and lock the doors. Having a ready mind is like that. You pack God's Word in your mind. You turn off wrong thinking. And you lock God's thinking into your mind.

Ramon was sad because his family might move. His dad was out of work and hoped there might be a job in another town. For Ramon, moving meant going to a new school and making new friends. Moving was the last thing he wanted to do. Ramon was sad so he talked to his pastor about it.

"Keep a willing mind," said Pastor Tom.

"But I don't want to move," complained Ramon.

"Trust God in this," said Pastor Tom. "Ask God to help your family stay in his plan. If it is best for you to move, God will help you handle it."

"Well, okay. I hope my dad's work won't be moved," replied Ramon. "But if things don't turn out the way I want, I'll be okay because I trust Jesus. I guess I can believe everything will work out for the best."

God wants you to have a willing mind. When you listen to God and obey him, you will be prepared for anything that might come your way.

Your Turn

1. Why does God want you to have a ready mind?
2. What will you do to get a ready mind?

_____

_____

_____

Prayer

Dear God, help me have a willing mind that trusts you. Amen.

Set Your Mind on God

My thoughts are not your thoughts, neither are your ways my ways.
– Isaiah 55:8

Mind Power
Make your mind ready for God's plan. In the head, draw a Bible, good things to do, attitudes to develop, and anything else that will help you prepare your mind and heart for God's plan.

Prayer
Dear God, I know that when I ask, you will help me have a mind that is focused on you. I am excited because you have a perfect plan for my life. Thank you! Amen.

Set Your Mind on God

My thoughts are not your thoughts, neither are your ways my ways.
– Isaiah 55:8

Baseball

Use the key to decode the baseballs to find out if your thoughts are like God's thoughts.

A	B	C	D	E	F	G	H	I	J	K	L	M
1	2	3	4	5	6	7	8	9	10	11	12	13

N	O	P	Q	R	S	T	U	V	W	X	Y	Z
14	15	16	17	18	19	20	21	22	23	24	25	26

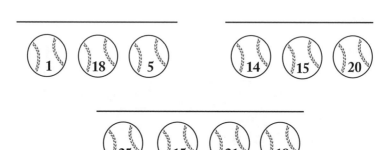

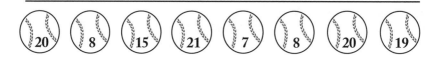

Prayer

Father God, sometimes I forget to ask you for help. I need to seek your thoughts on what to do. Amen.

Set Your Mind on God

My thoughts are not your thoughts, neither are your ways my ways.
– Isaiah 55:8

Doubt and Belief Maze

God doesn't want you to waste your time wondering what to do. He doesn't want you to doubt him. Complete the maze to find your way to a believing mind.

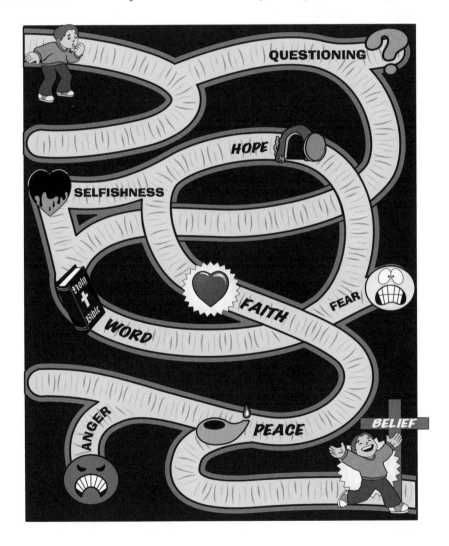

Prayer

God, give me a trusting and believing mind instead of one that wanders away from you. Help me trust you instead of worrying. Amen.

Be Careful What You Think

Consider carefully what you hear...with the measure
[of thought] you use, it will be measured to you.
– Mark 4:24

The Mind Patrol

Make the rounds. Walk the beat. Keep guard. Hold watch. Keep an eye out. Keep your eyes peeled. Be on your toes. Protect and watch over. Defend. Scout out. These words describe someone on patrol.

When Dave and Jon walked to school each day, they greeted the crosswalk patrol at the corner. The crosswalk patrol watched to make sure the kids crossed the street safely. The patrol was always watching and keeping an eye out for traffic.

The Bible says to be a guard for your mind. God wants you to patrol your thoughts. He wants you to watch for bad thoughts entering your mind so you can stop them right away. It's easy to get upset and focus on the troubles around you. Most of the time, it's how you think about what is happening that makes you feel sad and sometimes angry.

God wants you to be happy. That means you focus on the good things. When bad thoughts come, your patrol kicks them out and thinks about God's Word. Then you can ask God what he wants you to do.

Your Turn

1. How can you patrol your mind?
2. What Bible verses can you use to fight bad thoughts?

_____

_____

_____

_____

Prayer

God, teach me to patrol my mind. Help me think about the good things you bring. Remind me to think about your Word. Amen.

Be Careful What You Think

Consider carefully what you hear...with the measure
[of thought] you use, it will be measured to you.
– Mark 4:24

God's Whisper

God wants you to be ready to listen. Pretend God is whispering something in your ear. See if you can hear him by solving the crossword puzzle.

Down

1. God's Son

Across

2. What a valentine means
3. Opposite of me

Prayer

Dear God, help me keep my mind clear and ready to hear you speak to me. I'm listening! Amen.

Be Careful What You Think

*Consider carefully what you hear…with the measure
[of thought] you use, it will be measured to you.*
– Mark 4:24

Mind Patrol Log

Pick a day to patrol your mind. Write down what you are thinking every hour. At the end of the day, look at what you wrote. Did you think mostly good thoughts or mostly bad thoughts?

Noon _____

1:00 pm _____

2:00 pm _____

3:00 pm _____

4:00 pm _____

5:00 pm _____

6:00 pm _____

7:00 pm _____

8:00 pm _____

Prayer

God, help me keep my thoughts focused on you and what you would do as I go through my day. Amen.

Be Careful What You Think

Consider carefully what you hear…with the measure
[of thought] you use, it will be measured to you.
– Mark 4:24

The Humble Hero

One cold January day, an airplane with many people on board was taking off when it struck a bridge and sank into an icy river.

On the bridge, hundreds of people on their way home from work watched from their cars. Lenny was one of those people. Instead of just watching, he jumped into the water and saved a woman.

"Nobody else was doing anything," said Lenny. "I had to help."

Lenny was a humble hero. To "be humble" means your thoughts about yourself are not bigger than they should be. When you are selfish, it causes problems. The Bible warns about thinking you are too good. If you think and act like you are smarter, richer, and better than other people, you are not humble.

When the airplane crashed, many people watching had the "I and Me" problem. Maybe they thought the water was too cold. Perhaps they didn't want to get wet. Lenny thought more of others than himself. Afterward, he did not try to get credit. He was humble.

Loving Jesus will keep you from the "I and Me" problem. Ask God to help you think humbly rather than selfishly.

Your Turn

1. How can you become humble?
2.. Who do you know is humble and why do you think that?

_____

_____

_____

_____

Prayer

Dear Jesus, please make me humble and kind like you are. Amen.

Be Careful What You Think

Consider carefully what you hear…with the measure
[of thought] you use, it will be measured to you.
– Mark 4:24

The Heavenly Blog

Would you like to read about yourself in heaven's blog? Pretend you are famous in heaven for being a humble hero. Write your name on the computer screen and then write a story about yourself or draw a picture of you being a humble hero.

Prayer

God, I want to let people know that you are my hero. I want them to see you in me. Amen.

Be Careful What You Think

*Consider carefully what you hear...with the measure
[of thought] you use, it will be measured to you.*
– Mark 4:24

A Love Message
God wants his children to have minds filled with love for others.

What You Need
- a white crayon
  or a white wax candle
- watercolor paint
- a paintbrush or a cotton swab

What You Do
Use the crayon or candle and write a secret message of love to someone. Or you can draw a picture. Now use the watercolor paints and paint over your words or drawing. Your message will appear!

Prayer
Dear God, thank you that I can fill my mind with love instead of hate. Fill my thoughts and heart with love. Amen.

Be Careful What You Think

Consider carefully what you hear... with the measure
[of thought] you use, it will be measured to you.
– Mark 4:24

Worry-Watcher

Jesus said to look at the birds. They don't worry about what they will eat or drink or where they will build a nest. God takes care of them. Be a worry-watcher by catching yourself when you worry. Give your worry to God. Trust him to care for you.

Write your worries on the space by the bird in the tree. Pray and give each one to God.

Prayer

Dear God, you know when I am worried. Remind me to stop worrying and give it to you. Help me rest in your care and peace. Amen.

Be Wise

The foolishness of God is wiser than human wisdom.
– 1 Corinthians 1:25

Wise and Foolish Pigs

Once upon a time, there were three little pigs. One day their mother sent them into the world to make a living. She said, "Watch out for the big, bad wolf because he wants to eat you." She also told them, "Build your houses nice and strong. Then you will be safe from the wolf."

Two of the pigs were foolish builders. The first pig built his house with straw. The second pig built his house with sticks. The third pig was wise. He built his house with bricks.

As the mother pig said, the wolf came along and wanted to eat the little pigs. He huffed, he puffed, and he blew down the houses made of straw and sticks. Then the wolf huffed and puffed, and huffed and puffed again. He couldn't blow down the house of bricks.

Jesus tells a similar story in Matthew 7:24-25. "Everyone who hears these words of mine and puts them into practice is like a wise man who built his house on the rock. The rain came down, the streams rose, and the winds blew and beat against that house; yet it did not fall, because it had its foundation on the rock."

Build your life strong by using God's materials—his Word and prayer.

Your Turn

1. What happens if you build your life on the wrong things?
2. How can you build your life on strong things?

_____

_____

_____

_____

Prayer

Dear God, help me build my life around Jesus and your Word. Amen.

Be Wise

The foolishness of God is wiser than human wisdom.
– 1 Corinthians 1:25

Wise and Foolish Houses

Finish coloring the houses below. Which house is the wise person's house? Which house is the foolish person's house? Draw an X over the foolish person's house.

Prayer

Dear Lord, I want to live my life according to your wisdom. Please help me learn and use your Word. Then I know I will become wise. Amen.

Be Wise

The foolishness of God is wiser than human wisdom.
– 1 Corinthians 1:25

Opposite Words

Match the best opposites by drawing a line connecting them. Practice responding with the right words and in the right way so you will be wise when talking with someone who is upset.

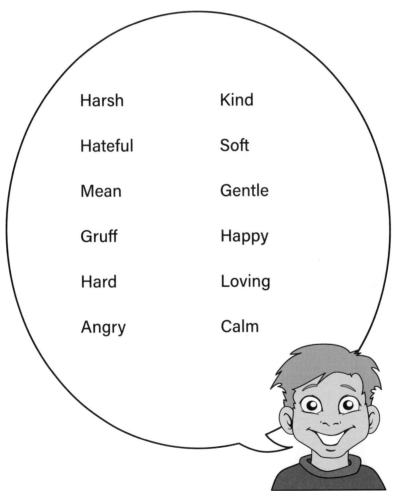

Harsh	Kind
Hateful	Soft
Mean	Gentle
Gruff	Happy
Hard	Loving
Angry	Calm

Prayer

Dear God, please help me to remember to answer people with kind words. Forgive me when I become angry and say mean things. Remind me to apologize and then speak the way You want me to. Amen.

Be Wise

The foolishness of God is wiser than human wisdom.
– 1 Corinthians 1:25

The Wisest Answer

"Get lost, you little donkey!" shouted Chad at his sister Ellie.

Ellie didn't want to shout back at Chad. She knew it would only make matters worse. So she smiled and acted like a donkey to be funny. "Hee haw, hee haw!" Ellie responded as she got on all fours.

Chad laughed. He wasn't angry anymore. The fighting ended.

Opposites work. Opposite words and actions often turn away evil. When someone shouts, you can whisper. When someone's words hurt, you can say something nice and healing. Angry words can be answered with calm, gentle words.

Proverbs 15:1 says, "A gentle answer turns away wrath." Many people hurt each other because of angry words. Jesus was hurt when he died for us. People said terrible things about him, but he didn't talk back. They hurt him, but he didn't hurt them back. Instead, he gave gentle answers and trusted God.

Jesus suffered for you and gave you a great example to follow. He was treated hatefully, but he didn't hate. He was mistreated, but he didn't return a harsh word. Jesus acted wisely.

Your Turn

1. How did Jesus answer his enemies?
2. How do you answer those who mistreat you with words?

_____

_____

_____

_____

Prayer

Dear God, please help me be kind and gentle like Jesus. Amen.

Be Wise

The foolishness of God is wiser than human wisdom.
– 1 Corinthians 1:25

Wise Highway Signs

There's a fork in the road up ahead. Which way will you go? Circle the highway signs that show the right way—God's way—to live.

Prayer

Dear God, help me understand your directions in the Bible. Make my heart willing to follow you. Amen.

Be Wise

The foolishness of God is wiser than human wisdom.
– 1 Corinthians 1:25

The Doctor's Bag

Jesus wants you to be like a doctor giving friendly word medicine to people. Don't forget to say friendly and pleasant words to people you meet. Draw a friendly face in the medicine bag below. Try extra hard to use pleasant and friendly words when you talk with people today.

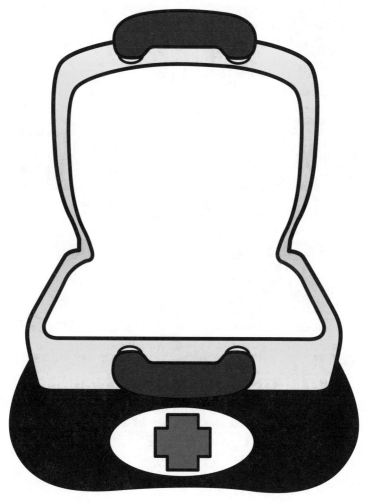

Prayer

Dear Lord, your words are like honey. My words are sour sometimes. Help me make people's hearts glad. Amen.

Be Wise

The foolishness of God is wiser than human wisdom.
– 1 Corinthians 1:25

Grocery Goodies

Fill the grocery sacks below with pleasant and friendly words you can speak to the people you see today. Do your best to use as many of these words as you can during the day.

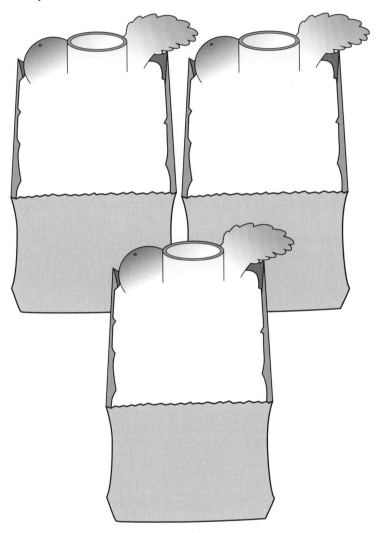

Prayer

Dear Jesus, it's good to know I can always depend on you. Help me be kind when I speak to my family, friends, and neighbors. Amen.

Love and Obey Jesus

And this is love: that we walk in obedience.
– 2 John 1:6

The Price of Disobedience

Bandit, a brown-and-white terrier, loved prowling the hills and streams near his house. The pup took great delight in exploring rabbit holes and trails. His master supplied him with good food, water, and a soft bed. Bandit needed to do only one thing: Be faithful to his master.

One day, Bandit was out playing when he saw a rabbit. At that moment, his master called to him. "Bandit, come home!"

Bandit immediately turned to run toward his master, but he stopped halfway there. I don't have to obey, he thought. It didn't matter to Bandit that the food in his dish came from his master. The The rabbit brushed by Bandit's leg, and the dog went after it. He made his choice between obeying his master or chasing the rabbit. Bandit ran away and got lost.

Jesus is like the master in this story because he provides you with the things you need in life. He cares for you and loves you. Listening to Jesus and obeying him keeps you within the safety of his love and care.

People are like Bandit because they want to do what they want to do. It is easy to get lost. When Bandit chased the rabbit, he got lost. In the same way, not obeying Jesus will get you lost.

Your Turn

1. What does disobedience do to your closeness with Jesus?
2. If you haven't obeyed Jesus, what should you do?

Prayer

Dear Jesus, keep me close to you. Help me listen and obey. Amen.

Love and Obey Jesus

And this is love: that we walk in obedience.
– 2 John 1:6

Rabbit Chase

Do you remember the story about the dog named Bandit? He didn't obey his master and instead ran after a rabbit. Follow the rabbit over the hill with your crayon. Cross out the wrong choices and circle the right choices.

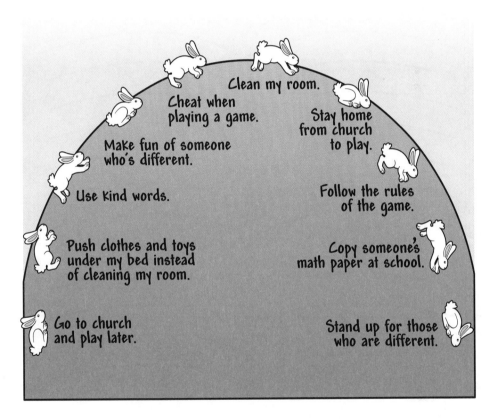

Clean my room.

Cheat when playing a game.

Stay home from church to play.

Make fun of someone who's different.

Use kind words.

Follow the rules of the game.

Push clothes and toys under my bed instead of cleaning my room.

Copy someone's math paper at school.

Go to church and play later.

Stand up for those who are different.

Prayer

Dear Jesus, I don't want to be like Bandit, always chasing after things. Help me listen to your voice and obey you. Amen.

Love and Obey Jesus

And this is love: that we walk in obedience.
– 2 John 1:6

Trust Journal

Use this journal page to write down some things you have trusted Jesus for. How did they turn out? You can also write down some things that you want to trust Jesus for. Pray about them. Come back to this page and write down how Jesus answered.

Prayer

Dear Jesus, I want to walk in obedience. I know that to do that, I need to trust you. Amen.

Love and Obey Jesus

And this is love: that we walk in obedience.
– 2 John 1:6

The Hard Thing

Something very odd happened one night as Jesus' disciples went across the Sea of Galilee: Jesus walked on top of the water to meet them! The disciples were terrified at first.

"It's a ghost!" they said, and cried out in fear.

Jesus called to them, saying, "Don't be afraid! It's Me, Jesus."

"If it's you," Peter said, "tell me to come to You on the water."

"Come," Jesus said.

Peter got out of the boat, walked on the water, and approached Jesus! But the wind and waves scared Peter. He began to sink. "Lord, save me!" cried Peter.

Jesus reached out his hand to catch Peter. "You of little faith. Why did you doubt?" Jesus said.

The rest of the men in the boat suddenly realized Jesus was God's Son. They worshipped him.

Reading a poem in front of the class, sleeping with the lights off, and trying out for the soccer team can be scary. Jesus wants you to trust him to help you.

Your Turn

1. What is the hardest thing for you to do?
2. What can you remember about Jesus when you are afraid?

_____

_____

_____

_____

Prayer

Dear Jesus, help me to trust you more. Make me into a person of faith so people will want to know you. Amen.

Love and Obey Jesus

And this is love: that we walk in obedience.
– 2 John 1:6

The Boat of Faith

Jesus can be trusted to help you with hard things. That's what Peter was learning when he got out of the boat to meet Jesus on top of the water. You can trust Jesus to be with you when something is scary. Draw a picture or write in the water about something that is scary. How can you let Jesus help you?

Prayer

Dear Jesus, like Peter, I want to trust you and go where you send me. Help me remember that you will always help me when I ask. Amen.

Love and Obey Jesus

And this is love: that we walk in obedience.
– 2 John 1:6

Trust Jesus Maze

Sometimes it can be scary to trust Jesus. Peter got scared when he walked on the water. Help the boy on the outside of the maze find his way to Jesus.

Prayer

Jesus, I want to always walk in obedience to you. Help me draw near to you and not be afraid. Amen.

Love and Obey Jesus

And this is love: that we walk in obedience.
– 2 John 1:6

Trusting Others

Write the names of three people you trust. Draw pictures of the people in your family you trust. Now pray and thank Jesus for them.

_____

_____

_____

_____

_____

_____

_____

_____

Prayer

Jesus, I am thankful that you have placed trustworthy people in my life. Help me be trustworthy for them as well. Amen.

Be like Jesus

Be strong and courageous. Do not be afraid; do not be discouraged,
for the LORD your God will be with you wherever you go.
–Joshua 1:9

The Boss of Fear

"Tell me again what you're going to do," Titus said to the doctor.

"I'm going to stick a small needle into your arm," the doctor said. He held up the needle. "A little of your blood will come through the needle and fill this small bottle."

Titus thought about the needle going into his arm and shivered.

The doctor said, "We have to find out if the medicine is helping you get well. Testing your blood is how we do that."

Titus asked, "Is there another way to test me??"

"No," the doctor said. "This is the only way."

"What if too much blood comes out?" Titus asked.

"I'm going to take care of you," the doctor said. "I'll be very careful."

"I'm scared," Titus said. "I guess I'm just a chicken."

"Everybody gets scared sometimes," the doctor said. "That doesn't mean you are a chicken."

"Brave people don't get scared," Titus said.

"Yes, they do," the doctor said. "But brave people don't let fear boss them around. They do the right thing even when they are afraid."

"I can do it," Titus said. "I'm scared, but I'm not going to let fear boss me around."

Your Turn

1. Can a person feel fear and courage at the same? Explain.
2. When were you scared? What happened? What will you do next time?

_____

_____

Prayer

God, by myself I'm not very brave. Help me when I get scared. I don't want fear to boss me around. Amen.

Be Like Jesus

Be strong and courageous. Do not be afraid; do not be discouraged,
for the LORD your God will be with you wherever you go.
– Joshua 1:9

Count the Ways You Served God Today

God is with you every day, everywhere you go. He is always giving you the chance
to show people that you love God. Count how many times you served God and
showed your love for him this week.

Saying "thank-you"

    1   **2**   **3**   _____

Helping someone

    1   **2**   **3**   _____

Listening to someone

    1   **2**   **3**   _____

Caring for nature

    1   **2**   **3**   _____

Taking care of your body

    1   **2**   **3**   _____

Prayer

God, thank you for being with me every day and everywhere I go. Help me
show my love for you by serving others. Amen.

Be Like Jesus

*Be strong and courageous. Do not be afraid; do not be discouraged,
for the LORD your God will be with you wherever you go.*
– Joshua 1:9

God Is with Me

Unscramble the words to find out what you can say when you get scared.

God is tihw em wherever I og so I ilwl not be rfadai.

Prayer

Dear Lord, when I am afraid, I choose to put my trust in you. I love you.
Amen.

Be Like Jesus

Be strong and courageous. Do not be afraid; do not be discouraged,
for the LORD your God will be with you wherever you go.
– Joshua 1:9

Door Jam

Jim rushed through the shop door. In his hand was a new baseball. His friends were waiting at the park. Jim didn't notice the woman behind him. She carried a baby in one arm and several bags in the other. The door crashed into her. She dropped her bags. Plastic baby bottles and rubber toys tumbled to the sidewalk. The scared baby cried.

Jim turned around in surprise. "I'm sorry!"

"It's okay," she said. "Sometimes I don't pay attention either."

He stooped to load the spilled stuff back into the bags. The woman comforted the crying child. As Jim picked up rattles and bottles, he thought about the woman's words. He hadn't been paying attention. He could have held the door for the woman. Even better, he could have carried the bags to her car to make her day a little easier. "Where are you parked?" he asked. "Let me help you."

The woman smiled and shifted the baby to her other hip. She led Jim to her car, and he put the bags inside.

As Jim pedaled his bike to the park, he decided to be more alert. When God gave him another chance to help, he was going to be ready!

Your Turn

1. How can you find ways to serve God?
2. What will you do today to help someone in your family?

_____

_____

_____

Prayer

God, I'm going to keep my eyes open for any chance You give me to help someone. Amen.

Be Like Jesus

Be strong and courageous. Do not be afraid; do not be discouraged,
for the LORD your God will be with you wherever you go.
– Joshua 1:9

A Prayer of Praise and Thanks
Fill in the blanks to write your prayer to God.

Dear God:
You are wonderful because
You _____
I'm sorry I _____
Thank You, God, for _____
_____
Please take care of _____
_____ and help
me to _____
_____ Amen

Be Like Jesus

Be strong and courageous. Do not be afraid; do not be discouraged,
for the LORD your God will be with you wherever you go.
– Joshua 1:9

You Can Serve God Today

Draw a picture of some way you have served God (or will serve God) by helping others.

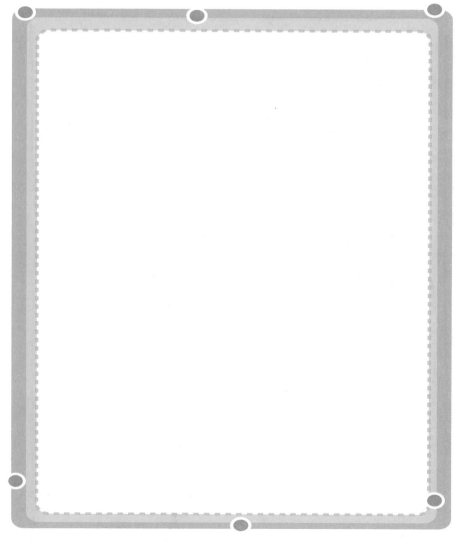

Prayer

Dear God, help me look for ways to help someone today. Amen.

Be Like Jesus

*Be strong and courageous. Do not be afraid; do not be discouraged,
for the LORD your God will be with you wherever you go.*
– Joshua 1:9

God's Spirit

Connect the dots to draw a symbol of God's Spirit.

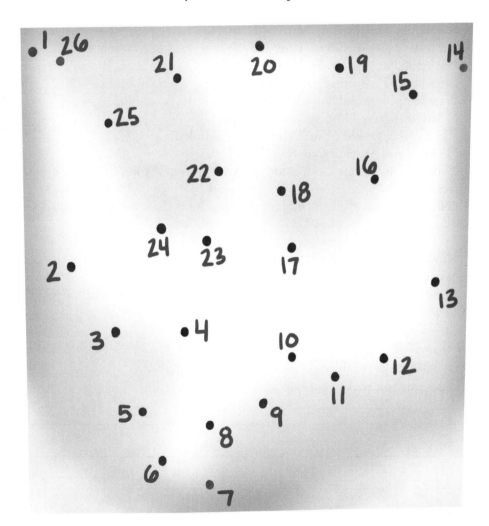

Prayer

Dear God, fill me up with your Holy Spirit. I want to help people and show
them how much you love them. Amen.

Be More Like God

Follow God's example, therefore, as dearly loved children and walk in the way of love, just as Christ loved us and gave himself up for us.
– Ephesians 5:1-2

Copy Cats

Nate and Josh were playing "Mirror." They stood facing each other. One person would make a face or strike a pose, and the other had to do it too.

Nate stood on one leg. So did Josh.

Nate flapped his arms like a bird flying in the sky. So did Josh.

Nate jumped up and down, doing jumping jacks. So did Josh.

"I love this game," Josh said and laughed.

"So do I," Nate said. "You're pretty good at imitating me."

"I wish I was better at imitating God," Josh said.

"Nobody can imitate God," Nate said with surprise. "You can't make storms or create worlds."

"No, I can't do stuff like that," Josh agreed. "But there is something God does that I can do. And the more I do this, the more I am like him."

"What is it?" Nate asked.

"Love," Josh said. "Of all the things God does, loving is the thing he does best. When I show love to somebody, I am imitating God."

"I never thought about that," Nate said. "It makes sense. We are God's children, and God wants us to be like him."

Your Turn

1. In what ways would you like to be more like God?
2. How can you make that happen?

_____

_____

_____

_____

Prayer

Wow, God! When I love others, I am becoming more like you. Amen.

Be More Like God

Follow God's example, therefore, as dearly loved children and walk in the way of love, just as Christ loved us and gave himself up for us.
– Ephesians 5:1-2

How Can You Be Holy?

The Bible tells us that God is holy and God wants us to be holy. What does it mean to be holy? Ask some adults what it means to be holy, and write their answers on the leaves of this tree. Which of these describes you?

Prayer

Dear Lord, I want to be holy because you love me so much, and I know you want me to be holy. Please help me live a holy life. Amen.

Be More Like God

Follow God's example, therefore, as dearly loved children and walk in the way of love, just as Christ loved us and gave himself up for us.
– Ephesians 5:1-2

Fish to Share

The Bible gives us good advice about what kind of people we can be to please God. One day Jesus was teaching many people, and they became hungry. A boy in the crowd had five loaves of bread and two cooked fish. He shared what he had with Jesus, and Jesus was pleased. He took the food and, with his help, there was enough to make sure no one went away hungry.

Write something on each fish that you can share. Are any of them hard for you to give to others? Color the fish with hard things to share red. Ask God to help you to be more willing to share this item with others. Then have fun coloring the other fish.

Prayer

Dear Jesus, I want to be like the boy in the Bible who shared his food. Sometimes it is hard for me to share, but I know You will help me have a willing heart. Thank you. Amen.

Be More Like God

Follow God's example, therefore, as dearly loved children and walk in the way of love, just as Christ loved us and gave himself up for us.
– Ephesians 5:1-2

The Unfunny Joker

"Hey, Hank!" Darin called. "Come on over. I've got a great joke."

Darin stood with some boys on the edge of the playground. He always had new jokes. Hank didn't think they were funny because they made fun of people. They were usually about people who didn't have skin like Darin's and were from other countries. Sometimes his jokes were about people who couldn't walk or see.

Darin said he didn't mean any harm, that they were just jokes. But Hank felt uncomfortable. He remembered his preacher had talked about being holy. "Every Christian is called to be holy. That means you belong to God. It means doing things God's way instead of going along with the crowd."

Darin and the boys ran over to Hank. He took a deep breath. "Darin, I like you but not your jokes. If you want to play ball or something, count me in. But leave me out of listening to jokes that make fun of people."

As Hank walked away, Darin said something Hank couldn't hear and the boys laughed. Maybe they were laughing at him, but Hank didn't care. Pleasing God was a lot more important.

Your Turn

1. What did Hank do that was brave?
2. "What is a way you can please God?

_____

_____

_____

Prayer

God, being holy isn't easy. I'm going to need your help. Amen.

Be More Like God

Follow God's example, therefore, as dearly loved children and walk in the way of love, just as Christ loved us and gave himself up for us.
– Ephesians 5:1-2

Search Your Heart

Look for these words in the word search. Are these the things people see in your heart?

FORGIVE   SORRY   JESUS
LOVE   KIND

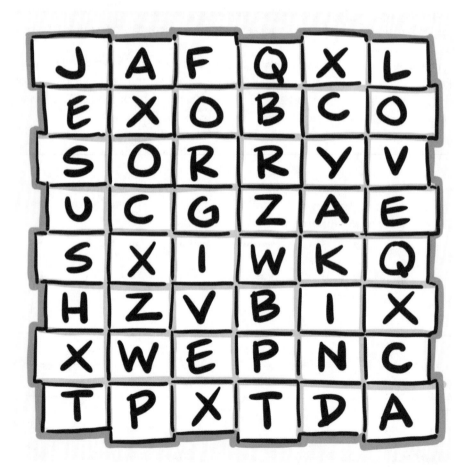

Prayer

Dear God, I know you want me to love others. Show me how to forgive people when they do something wrong when I am with them. Amen.

Be More Like God

Follow God's example, therefore, as dearly loved children and walk in the way of love, just as Christ loved us and gave himself up for us.
– Ephesians 5:1-2

What Makes you Strong

All the pieces of the puzzle add up to a good, strong Christian. Color the puzzle pieces green if they says something you are working to do. Color the puzzle pieces red if they are something you do well now.

Prayer

Jesus, you are gentle and kind. Please help me be more like you. Amen.

Be More Like God

Follow God's example, therefore, as dearly loved children and walk in the way of love, just as Christ loved us and gave himself up for us.
– Ephesians 5:1-2

God's Love

Color the puzzle pieces that have an asterisk (*) blue. Use the blue letters to complete the sentence.

Remember to _____ _____ _____ _____

others the way God loves me.

Prayer

Dear God, with your help I know I can love people like you. Amen.

Stay on Track

Listen, my son, and be wise, and set your heart on the right path.
– Proverbs 23:19

The Right Path

"Jordan, did he tag you?" Dan called. "Were you safe?"

Both baseball teams gathered around to hear Jordan's answer.

"I know I tagged him," said the kid playing third base. "But he might have touched the base first. I couldn't tell."

"So, were you safe?" Dan asked again. He was captain of Jordan's team, and he hated to lose. If Jordan was out at third, his team lost.

Jordan thought, *Dan will be so angry if that happened, he'd probably yell at me for not running faster.* If Jordan was safe, his team would probably win. The next batter was a good hitter. Jordan, coming from third base, might score the winning run!

There was only one problem. Jordan knew the third baseman had tagged him before he reached the base. Jordan knew he was out, but no one else did. It would be so easy to lie about it. But he knew that telling a little lie now would make it easier to tell a bigger lie later. He remembered the Bible encourages people to be honest and honor God.

Jordan decided to do the smart thing. "He tagged me. I'm out."

Your Turn

1. Why did Jordan tell the truth?
2. When is it hard for you to tell the truth? What do you usually do?

_____

_____

_____

_____

Prayer

God, cheating and lying might be easier and make me look better, but my heart won't be clean and I won't look good in your eyes. Amen.

Stay on Track

Listen, my son, and be wise, and set your heart on the right path.
– Proverbs 23:19

Be Joyful!

Cross out the letters B, P, Q, and X to decode the message. Will you live by these words every day? [Message = I will give thanks and rejoice every day of my life.]

Prayer

Lord, please help me develop the habit of being joyful no matter what is going on. Amen.

Stay on Track

Listen, my son, and be wise, and set your heart on the right path.
– Proverbs 23:19

Staying on Track

Keep this train on the right track by crossing off the cars that would be bad decisions.

Prayer

God, I sure don't want to make bad decisions. Help me keep my heart on the right track. Amen.

Stay on Track

Listen, my son, and be wise, and set your heart on the right path..
– Proverbs 23:19

The Bright Side

"What did you get on your English test?" Ryan asked.

"A lousy grade," Evan said cheerfully.

"I bombed too," Ryan said. "Why are you so happy?"

Evan put the test in his backpack. "I'm not happy because I got a bad grade. I'm happy in spite of the bad grade."

The boys walked out the school and lined up for their bus.

"I don't get it," Ryan said.

"A low grade is bad," Evan said. "But I have things I'm happy about."

"Like what?" Ryan asked.

"It's only September," Evan said. "I have time to improve my grade. Also, I know why I got a bad grade. I forgot to study. That means I can do better next time. I am getting good grades in math."

"I think I understand," Ryan said, smiling.

"Besides," Evan added, "will it make my grade any better if I feel crummy about it? Feeling bad will just make me discouraged."

The Bible says to rejoice always. There are two ways of choosing joy in bad times. One way is to remember the good things in life and give God thanks. Another way is to hang on to hope. Joy and hope go together.

Your Turn

1. How can you find joy when you are having a hard day?

2. Hope looks forward with a positive attitude. What do you hope for?

_____

_____

_____

_____

Prayer

God, today is not going well. Give me hope for tomorrow. Amen.

Stay on Track

Listen, my son, and be wise, and set your heart on the right path.
– Proverbs 23:19

Look at Your Face

When people look at you, do they see an angry face or a kind face? Draw an angry face on one of the boys and draw a kind face on the other boy. Ask God to help you wear a kind face.

Prayer

God, I want to get along well with people. Remind me to always be kind. Amen.

Stay on Track

Listen, my son, and be wise, and set your heart on the right path.
– Proverbs 23:19

Pop the Balloons

God wants you to be patient when you face tough times. He will help you. Pop the balloons by marking them with an "X" if they are not a good way to wait. Color the balloons that show patience and trust in God.

Prayer

God, I know that you are working to make things better for me so I can wait without complaining or moping. Thank you. Amen.

Stay on Track

Listen, my son, and be wise, and set your heart on the right path.
– Proverbs 23:19

A Rule to Live By

Is fighting a good way or a bad way to settle things? God wants us to live peaceably with others. Look at the pictures. Can you figure out the message?

Copy the page and put it on your wall to remind you every day to live that way.

Prayer

God, teach me to be peaceable, especially with the people who bug me. Amen.

Hold Tight to God's Love

Let the message of Christ dwell among you richly.
– Colossians 3:16

Start Sprouting

The Bible shares a story about planting that will remind you of the good news of God's love.

A farmer went out to spread seeds in his field. Some of the seeds fell along the path where the farmer was walking. Those seeds never grew because birds ate them. Other seeds fell on stony soil, where the dirt was very thin. Those seeds sprouted and grew, but there was no room for the roots to grow. When the day got hot, those plants died because their roots could not reach water. Some of the seeds fell into places where weeds and thorns were growing. The thorns were so tough that they left little room for the new seeds to grow. Pretty soon the new seeds died because the weeds crushed and starved them.

Some seeds fell on good, rich soil. The rain fell on those seeds, and the sun warmed them. The seeds grew and grew. At harvest, those plants produced great amounts of grain.

Jesus wants you to be like the seeds that fell on good soil. As God's good news grows in your heart, you will grow more like Jesus and you will share Jesus with your friends.

Your Turn

1. If you were a seed, where would you want to be planted?
2. How can you remind yourself of God's love every day?

_____

_____

_____

_____

Prayer

God, I want to be like seeds in good soil. I'm going to listen to your good news and grow in you. Amen.

Hold Tight to God's Love

Let the message of Christ dwell among you richly.
– Colossians 3:16

Helping Jesus

Did you know that if you help someone, it is like helping Jesus? That means you can find ways to help Jesus everywhere. How many times can you find "JESUS" in the word search?

Prayer

Jesus, please help me see people who need my help. I'm happy to help them because when I do, my love for you shows. Amen.

Hold Tight to God's Love

Let the message of Christ dwell among you richly.
– Colossians 3:16

Nothing Is Too Little

God can use anything—large or small—to do his work. Here is a picture story about little things that made a difference. Figure out the story by numbering the pictures so they are in the correct order.

Prayer

God, I am not big or strong yet, but I know you can use me for your work. I am a willing worker! Amen.

Hold Tight to God's Love

Let the message of Christ dwell among you richly.
– Colossians 3:16

Giving a Hand

Here is a retelling of a story Jesus told (Matthew 25:31-46).

Someday the Son of Man [Jesus] will sit on his throne and gather the people of the world before him. The King will tell some people to stand at his right hand. He will say, "When I was sick, you came to see me. When I was in jail, you came to visit me. When I was hungry, you brought me food. Come and receive God's blessings."

Those people will say, "Lord, when did we see you hungry or sick or in jail? When did we visit you or feed you?"

The King will say, "Whenever you did kind things to people who needed help, it was as if you did them for me."

The King will gather the other people on his left. He will say, "When I was sick or cold or hungry or in jail, you did nothing to help me. God is disappointed with you."

Those people will say, "But, Lord, we never saw you hungry or cold or sick or in jail."

The King will say, "If you passed by anyone in need, it was the same as if you passed me by."

Those who had never helped felt great sorrow.

Your Turn

1. When you see someone who needs help, what do you do?
2. When you help someone, do you think of Jesus? Explain.

_____

_____

_____

_____

Prayer

Jesus, I will show my love for you by loving and helping people. Amen.

Hold Tight to God's Love

Let the message of Christ dwell among you richly.
– Colossians 3:16

Pray Each Day

One of the ways you can know Jesus better is to pray every day. Do you talk to Jesus every day? Or do you forget to pray? Or do you get too busy? How can you get in the habit of praying? Set aside a regular time and place to pray. Here is a list to help you get started. Fill in the list and use it for a week. If it helps, use it again and again.

How many times I want to pray each day:

_____

The best time for me to pray:

_____

The best place for me to pray:

_____

Things I want to pray about each day:

_____

My prayer partner:

_____

Prayer

Lord, I want to talk to you every day but sometimes I forget. Thank you for helping me find ways to remember. Amen.

Hold Tight to God's Love

Let the message of Christ dwell among you richly.
– Colossians 3:16

Make Your Own Comic Strip

Do you remember reading the story about the seeds? Well, get your pencils, crayons, and markers. You are going to turn the story of the seeds into a mini comic book. Fill the panels with pictures to tell the story. Hint: You might make the farmer look like Jesus:

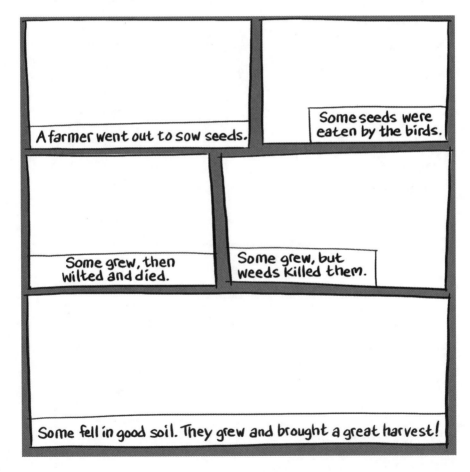

A farmer went out to sow seeds.

Some seeds were eaten by the birds.

Some grew, then wilted and died.

Some grew, but weeds killed them.

Some fell in good soil. They grew and brought a great harvest!

Prayer

God, I want to be like the seed that fell in the good soil and brought a great harvest! I want your Word to grow in my heart so I can tell others the good news about Jesus. Amen.

Hold Tight to God's Love

Let the message of Christ dwell among you richly.
– Colossians 3:16

Find the Good Soil

God wants you to grow in him by reading your Bible and praying every day. Help the boy get to the right field to plant the seeds so they'll grow into healthy plants.

Prayer

Dear God, help me water the seeds of life I get from learning about you. I want to grow stronger in you every day. Amen.

Loving God Is the Best

Store up for yourselves treasures in heaven, where moths and vermin do not destroy, and where thieves do not break in and steal.
– Matthew 6:20

Best of All

Here's a paraphrase of a story Jesus told (Matthew 13:45-56).

A merchant made his living buying and selling pearls. Traders came to sell bags of pearls they gathered from the ocean. The merchant would buy only the finest pearls for his store. One day a traveler came. He went into the pearl shop and laid a cloth bag on the counter. "Open it," he said.

The merchant opened the bag. His eyes grew wide and his mouth fell open. Inside was the largest pearl he had ever seen. The pearl was perfect in every way—shiny, white, round, and huge.

"This pearl is worth a great deal of money," said the merchant. "Come back in one week, and I will buy it from you." Then the merchant sold all the pearls in his store to raise money. When the traveler returned a week later, there was not one pearl left in the shop.

The merchant took all the money he had made and gave it to the traveler for the great pearl. When the great pearl belonged to him, the merchant's heart filled with joy.

That's how much the merchant loved the beautiful pearl. And that's how much you should love God.

Your Turn

1. Do your friends know how important God is?
2. How can you show them how important God is to you?

_____

_____

_____

_____

Prayer

God, you are Number One with me. I love you. Amen.

Loving God Is the Best

Store up for yourselves treasures in heaven, where moths and vermin do not destroy, and where thieves do not break in and steal.
– Matthew 6:20

Most of All

Do you remember the story of the merchant who bought the pearl? The merchant loved the great pearl more than everything else. Do you love Jesus that way? To show that Jesus is the King in your life, decorate the crown, staff, and throne for him. Use bright colors and add lots of jewels. Be sure to put in some pearls!

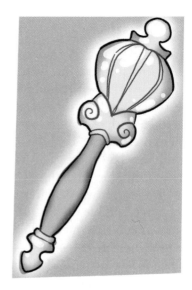

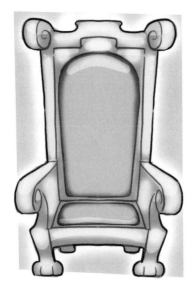

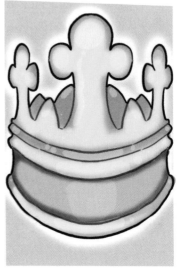

Prayer

Jesus, you are my Pearl of great price. You are King of my life. I love you more than anything. I am glad you are my Lord and Savior. Amen.

Loving God Is the Best

Store up for yourselves treasures in heaven, where moths and vermin do not destroy, and where thieves do not break in and steal.
– Matthew 6:20

Finding Sheep

Does Jesus love you? Absolutely! In the puzzle, cross out all the F's, the L's, and the W's to find out what Jesus said that shows how much he loves you.

Prayer

God, sometimes I wander off to places where I shouldn't go. Thanks for loving me anyway. I know you will always bring me back to you. Amen.

Loving God Is the Best

Store up for yourselves treasures in heaven, where moths and vermin do not destroy, and where thieves do not break in and steal.
– Matthew 6:20

Better Than Money

Here's another paraphrase of a story Jesus told (Luke 12:16-21)!

A rich man owned a big farm. Each year he raised crops of barley and wheat. The soil was very good, and the farmer harvested many baskets of grain. He had so many crops that it was much more than he could use. His barns filled up, but there was still more grain.

The rich man thought, This farm makes so much grain! If I can store it all, I will be rich forever. I'll never have to work again. He decided to build bigger barns. He called in many workers and told them to build bigger barns. The rich man believed that when the new barns were filled with crops, his future was safe and secure.

But he was wrong.

God said to him, "You foolish man! You are going to die tonight. Everything you have will be given to someone else. What good will your riches do you now?"

Instead of filling his life with new barns, the rich man should have been filling his life with God's love and wisdom.

Your Turn

1. If you met the rich man in this story, what would you tell him?
2. Do you enjoy your things more than you enjoy God?

_____

_____

_____

_____

Prayer

God, my stuff will be with me until it breaks or gets lost. You will be with me forever. Hooray! Amen.

Loving God Is the Best

Store up for yourselves treasures in heaven, where moths and vermin do not destroy, and where thieves do not break in and steal.
– Matthew 6:20

Bigger Barns

Oops! The story Jesus told about the rich man has gotten some of the words messed up. The wrong words are underlined. Cross out the incorrect word and write the correct word above it. The right word will rhyme with the wrong word. If you need help, you can find this story in your Bible in Luke 12:16-21.

The *hound* of a certain rich man produced a good *slop*. He thought to himself, "What shall I do? I have no place to store my *mops*."

Then he said, "This is what I'll do. I will tear down my *yarns* and build bigger ones, and there I will store all my *rain* and my *woods*. And I'll say to myself, 'You have *twenty* of good things laid up for many *ears*. Take life easy; eat, drink and be *hairy*."

But God said to him, "You *drool*! This very night your *knife* will be demanded from you. Then who will get what you have prepared for yourself?"

Prayer

Dear Lord, I know you are better than anything else in my life. You forgave my sins and gave me eternal life with you. Amen.

Loving God Is the Best

Store up for yourselves treasures in heaven, where moths and vermin do not destroy, and where thieves do not break in and steal.
– Matthew 6:20

Be a Good Neighbor

Read the story of a good neighbor in Luke 10:25-37 or Week 17, Day 4. Loving God includes storing up treasure in heaven by being a good friend. Think about how the people in the story felt. Match the words on the left to pictures from the story on the right. You might match the word to more than one picture.

Frightened
Lonely
Hurt
Hateful
Sorry
Selfish
Worried
Too Busy
Yuck!
Thankful
I don't want
to get dirty

Robbers beat the man and left him hurt and lying in a ditch.

The minister and church worker saw the man, but left him in the ditch to die.

The Samaritan took the hurt man to a place where he would be taken care of.

The man was alive because someone had taken the time to help him.

Prayer

Jesus, I don't want to pass by people who need help. Open m eyes to ways to help. Amen.

Loving God Is the Best

Store up for yourselves treasures in heaven, where moths and vermin do not destroy, and where thieves do not break in and steal.
– Matthew 6:20

Talking to Jesus

No matter how hard you try to follow Jesus, sometimes you will make mistakes. One great thing about loving Jesus is that he is always ready to forgive you and love you. Help the boy find Jesus. Watch out for the roadblocks along the way. Only one path leads back to Jesus.

Prayer

Dear God, I never want to wander away from you. But if I ever do, touch my heart and lead me back to you. Amen.

God Forgives You

God, have mercy on me, a sinner.
– Luke 18:13

God Sees Your Heart

Jesus used stories to teach people. This paraphrased story is about praying (Luke 18:10-14).

Two men went to the temple to pray. One man was a Pharisee. He spent a lot of time in the temple and knew all the Jewish religion's laws. Everyone thought he was extraordinary—including him.

The other man was a tax collector. In those days, tax collectors represented the Romans. Tax collectors often cheated their fellow Jews. Most people hated tax collectors.

These two men were praying. The Pharisee was proud. He stood and prayed out loud, "God, thank you for making me such a wonderful person. Look at that tax collector. I am much better than he is."

The tax collector was different. He was ashamed of his mistakes. He got on his knees and turned his face toward the floor. He didn't stand in front of people. He didn't act like he was the best and never made mistakes. He prayed, "God, I am such a sinner. Please forgive me."

Jesus asked his followers, "Which man pleased God with his prayer? It was not the proud Pharisee. God was pleased by the honest prayer of the tax collector."

Your Turn

1. Should people brag when they talk to God? Explain.
2. What's a way you can show you have a humble and honest heart?

_____

_____

_____

_____

Prayer

God, when I mess things up I'm going to tell you the truth about it. I'm never going to pretend when I'm talking to you. Amen.

God Forgives You

God, have mercy on me, a sinner.
– Luke 18:13

Forgiven and Forgiving

Here is a prayer Jesus taught. This prayer reminds you to ask for forgiveness from God and to give forgiveness to others. Use the code-breaker to figure out what the prayer says.

ULITREV FH ULI

WLRMT DILMT

ZH DV ULITREV

LGSVIH

A is Z	H is S	O is L	V is E
B is Y	I is R	P is K	W is D
C is X	J is Q	Q is J	X is C
D is W	K is P	R is I	Y is B
E is V	L is O	S is H	Z is A
F is U	M is N	T is G	
G is T	N is M	U is F	

Prayer

God, please help me to quickly forgive others. I am glad you forgive me, and I want to do the same when someone does something bad. Amen.

God Forgives You

God, have mercy on me, a sinner.
– Luke 18:13

Forgiveness

When you forgive someone, it means you are no longer angry about what that person did to you. Sometimes it is hard to forgive people, but keep doing it because God forgives you when you do wrong.

Use these writing boards to practice forgiveness. On the blackboard, use a black crayon or marker to color over the sins and make them disappear. When you forgive, you have made bad feelings disappear.

On the whiteboard, write the names of people you need to forgive. Ask God to help you do that and then pray for them.

Prayer

God, please help me forgive the people who have hurt me or made me sad. Amen.

God Forgives you

God, have mercy on me, a sinner.
– Luke 18:13

IOU

Jesus told a story about forgiveness (Matthew 18:23-35).

Once there was a rich, powerful ruler who had many servants. The ruler remembered that one of his servants owed him money. He called in the servant and said, "You owe me millions of dollars. It's time to pay up."

The servant said, "Master, I don't have enough. Have pity on me."

The master said, "I forgive you all the millions you owe me. I will not punish you. I will forget about the money you owe me."

The servant was very happy. As he returned to his house, he ran into a neighbor who owed him a a few dollars.

"Pay me the money you owe me!" the servant demanded.

The neighbor said, "I cannot pay you right now. Please give me a little time. I will pay you later."

The servant said no. He called the police, and the neighbor was sent to jail.

When the king found out about this, he called in the servant. "I forgave you millions of dollars, but you threw your neighbor into jail because he owed you a few dollars. Now I will not forget the money you owe me. You will go to jail until you pay back every penny."

Your Turn

1. Why did the king have his servant put in jail?
2. When you forgive someone, how do you feel?

_____

_____

_____

_____

Prayer

God, when people upset me, help me focus on you and forgive them the way you forgive me. Amen.

God Forgives You

God, have mercy on me, a sinner.
– Luke 18:13

The Way to Pray

Each one of the sentences is a prayer. Read each prayer and choose the traffic sign that matches it. If you think it is a good way to pray, color the "GO" sign green. If you think it is not so good, but not too bad, color the "SLOW" sign yellow. If you think it is a bad way to pray, color the "STOP" sign red.

1) God, thank you for taking care of me.

2) I don't need you much, God. I'm pretty cool all by myself.

3) Sometimes I need a little help, God.

4) God, I'm mad at Bobby. Crash his bike.

5) Please take care of my friends, God.

6) I don't want to study. Help me with the test, God.

Prayer

God, I want my prayers to reflect your heart. Amen.

God Forgives You

God, have mercy on me, a sinner.
– Luke 18:13

Your Sins Are Gone!

When you tell God you are sorry for making a mistake and not following his ways, he forgives you completely. Get your Bible and look up Psalm 103:12. Write the Scripture verse across the map of the world.

Prayer

Lord, I am so grateful that when I pray and ask you to forgive me, I can be sure you will. Thank you. Amen.

God Forgives You

God, have mercy on me, a sinner.

– Luke 18:13

Prayer Zones

One way you can get closer to God is by praying daily. When you pray for others, God is pleased. He will answer in his perfect way. Describe the way you usually pray.

Try these "prayer zones" during this week.
Which one did you like best?

ZONE 1:
Daily quiet time prayer

ZONE 2:
Short prayers before meals and sleeping

ZONE 3:
Sudden, unplanned prayers during the day

Prayer

God, I know that when I pray, you listen and answer. Help me share with you everything that is on my mind. Amen.

God Has Big Plans for you

*Let your light shine before others, that they may see
your good deeds and glorify your Father in heaven.*
– Matthew 5:16

Brighten Up

Jose swung his hand through the evening air and caught a firefly. Aaron scooped one from the air too. Soft light from the glowing body poked between his fingers. After a moment, he opened his hand, and the brown bug flew away.

"How do they shine like that?" Aaron asked.

"Some kind of chemicals, I guess," Jose said.

"I wish I could shine like that," Aaron said.

"You can," Jose said. "Jesus said believers like you and me are supposed to be the light of the world."

"What does that mean?" Aaron asked as a bug circled his head.

"We can make the world a brighter place by telling people about Jesus and doing good things," Jose explained. "When I help Mrs. Kravitz with groceries, I'm brightening her day. When I help Coach put away equipment, I'm shining light into his life."

"I get it," Aaron said. "When I work with my little sister on her science project, I'm shining light on her."

"That's it!" Jose agreed. "Jesus shines his love into our lives, and we reflect some of it onto others."

your Turn

1. How do people shine with the love of Jesus?
2. How do you shine for Jesus?

_____

_____

_____

_____

Prayer

God, shine your love on me, and I'll shine it on everybody I meet. Amen.

God Has Big Plans for You

Let your light shine before others, that they may see your good deeds and glorify your Father in heaven.
– Matthew 5:16

Share the Good News

People who are hard of hearing or deaf often use American sign language. Use the key to crack the code and discover an important message:

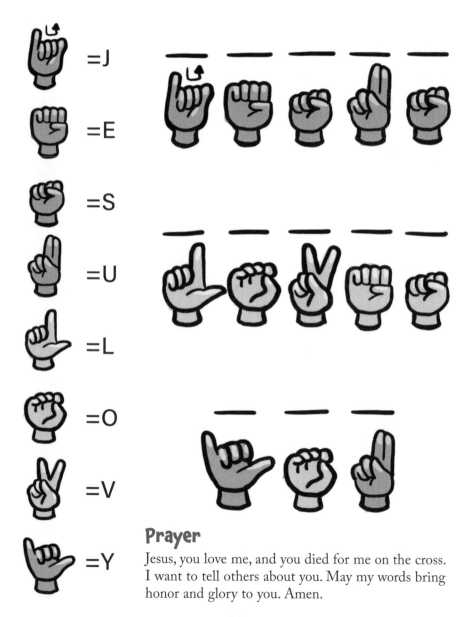

Prayer

Jesus, you love me, and you died for me on the cross. I want to tell others about you. May my words bring honor and glory to you. Amen.

God Has Big Plans for You

*Let your light shine before others, that they may see
your good deeds and glorify your Father in heaven.*
– Matthew 5:16

How You Can Shine

The following sentences show ways you can shine with the love of Jesus. Choose the one you like best from each pair.

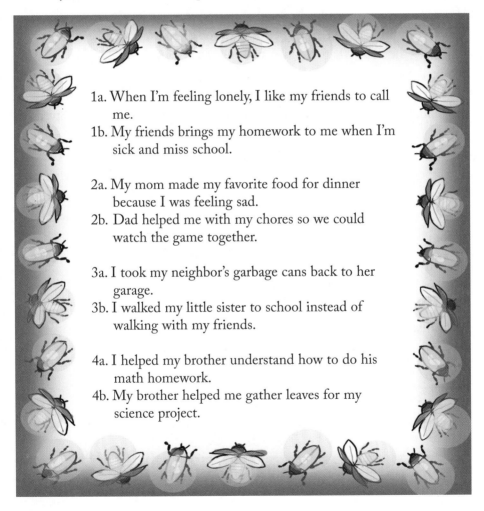

1a. When I'm feeling lonely, I like my friends to call me.
1b. My friends brings my homework to me when I'm sick and miss school.

2a. My mom made my favorite food for dinner because I was feeling sad.
2b. Dad helped me with my chores so we could watch the game together.

3a. I took my neighbor's garbage cans back to her garage.
3b. I walked my little sister to school instead of walking with my friends.

4a. I helped my brother understand how to do his math homework.
4b. My brother helped me gather leaves for my science project.

Prayer

God, I want to shine for you. When people know me, I want them to see something different about me. I will tell them that the difference is because I love you. Amen.

God Has Big Plans for you

*Let your light shine before others, that they may see
your good deeds and glorify your Father in heaven.*
– Matthew 5:16

Sharing Honey

Honey bees spend their time looking for the sweet nectar inside flower blossoms. When a bee finds a flower, it gathers a tiny drop of sugary nectar. The bee carries it back to the hive, where he lives with hundreds of other bees. The nectar is broken down and stored as honey to feed the bees when the weather turns cold.

When a honey bee finds a field of flowers, it flies back to the hive and shares the good news. Bees can't talk, so they dance. A bee wiggles his rear and turns in circles. The other bees understand the dance, and they can now find the flower meadow.

Honey bees don't keep good news a secret. They share it with others. God wants you to share the way honey bees do. You have good news—Jesus loves you and died to take away your sins. When you believe in Jesus, you are part of God's forever family.

Would it be right to keep such good news a secret? That's why you tell others about Jesus, invite friends to Sunday school, and go to church.

Your Turn

1. Pick two friends to talk to about Jesus this week.
2. Thank the person who told you about Jesus.

Prayer

God, I want everyone to know about you. Amen.

God Has Big Plans for You

Let your light shine before others, that they may see
your good deeds and glorify your Father in heaven.
– Matthew 5:16

What Comes Out of Your Mouth

It's a good idea to practice using words for good things so you can share Jesus easier. Look at the words and draw a picture in each box that fits the caption.

Don't worry. Everyone makes mistakes sometimes.

Hey, you are really good at that. Can you show me how you do it?

Thank you for helping me. Maybe I can help you next time.

Prayer

God, sometimes bad words and thoughts come out of my mouth. Please help me to use all my words for good. Amen.

God Has Big Plans for You

*Let your light shine before others, that they may see
your good deeds and glorify your Father in heaven.*
– Matthew 5:16

Oh the Places You Can Go!

With God anything is possible. Where do you think you might go in life? Draw a path on the map below that includes the places you might go and the things you might do.

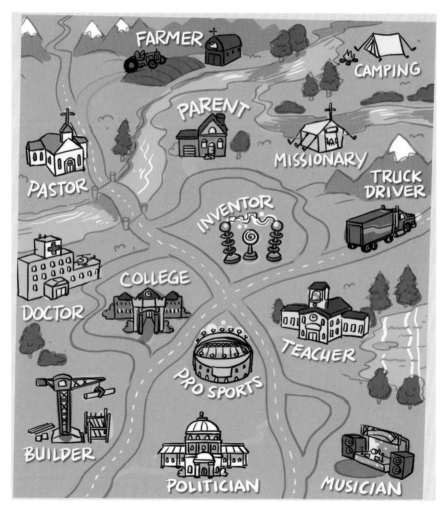

Prayer

God, I've grown a lot since I was a baby. I can't wait to see what you have planned for me next. Amen.

God Has Big Plans for You

Let your light shine before others, that they may see
your good deeds and glorify your Father in heaven.
– Matthew 5:16

Can You Picture It?

Draw a picture that shows how you will share Jesus with your friends. Will you share while playing baseball? While eating lunch? On your way to or from school?

Prayer

God, my light will shine for you when I praise you and when I do good deeds. I want to be your shining light that others can see. Amen.

Let Jesus Show you the Way

"Come, follow me," Jesus said.
– Matthew 4:19

Walking with Jesus

Jeremy found an old board on the ground and turned it over. Underneath the board, ants ran in all directions. A two-inch long millipede marched across the wet dirt. It was like a hairy black worm with many legs that rose and fell like a slow wave along its body.

Jeremy wondered how the millipede kept those legs working together. Sometimes on the soccer field, Jeremy couldn't make his two legs work with each other. What would it be like to have hundreds of legs?

"Hey, little millipede," Jeremy said. "You can go through tall grass, up a tree, down a hole. I guess you never fall down." The millipede came to a pebble. Its body flowed over the rock like a ripple of water.

"You're good at walking, but you don't know where you're going. You wander around looking for food and hiding from birds." The millipede continued on its way.

"I only have two legs," Jeremy said, "but at least I know where I'm going. I'm following Jesus. I walk with him. I read his Word. I live the way he teaches. I know my life is going somewhere. Jesus has a plan for me."

Your Turn

1. How is your life different because you follow Jesus?

_____

_____

_____

_____

Prayer

Jesus, I love this game of follow the leader we're playing together. You are the leader, and I am your follower. Amen.

Let Jesus Show You the Way

"Come, follow me," Jesus said.
– Matthew 4:19

A Tracker

Can you match the footprints to the animals that made them? Draw a line from the animal to its footprints. Now follow the instructions to find the secret message.

Change the 1's to E's; the 2's to I's; the 3's to O's; and the 4's to U's

2'm g32ng t3 f3ll3w J1s4s

_____ _____ __ _____ _____

Prayer

Jesus, I want to follow you. Keep me close to you always. When I stray, please bring me back to you. Amen.

Let Jesus Show You the Way

"Come, follow me," Jesus said.
– Matthew 4:19

Choices

Do you ever get distracted and make a poor choice? Let's practice some very good decisions. Circle the choice you think Jesus would want to do. Is that the choice you would make too?

1a. Go to a friend's birthday party when he invites you.

1b. Sleep in and skip church.

2a. Help your mom and dad with chores.

2b. Hide your candy so you don't have to share it with your brother or sister.

3a. Keep the cool pencil you borrowed from the kid next to you in math.

3b. Give a friend half of your sandwich because he forgot his lunch.

Prayer

God, please help me to stop and think before I make choices. I want to make choices that are good and will please you. Amen.

Let Jesus Show You the Way

"Come, follow me," Jesus said.
– Matthew 4:19

Smarter Than a Bug

It was after dark when Connor got home from playing basketball at his friend's house. As he climbed the porch steps, he noticed moths circling the bright light. Whenever the porchlight was on, some were drawn to the glow. Connor didn't know what moths did with their time. Maybe they looked for food. Whatever moths did, there must be something better than flying around and around a light bulb.

Dumb moths, Connor thought. What a silly way to live. The light distracted them from living fully. Then Connor remembered how he got distracted sometimes. Last Sunday, he'd told his mom he didn't want to go to church. A new show was on TV that his friends said was good. Connor had never seen it because it was on during church.

His mother recorded the program so he could watch it after church. When he did, he decided Mighty Astrobots wasn't that good. He felt silly that he'd almost let a TV show get in the way of worshipping God.

Your Turn

1. What things distract you from paying attention to Jesus?
2. What will you do next time to get your mind back on Jesus?

_____

_____

_____

_____

Prayer

God, I don't want to be like a moth. I want to be like a tree growing toward the sun. I want to reach out to you. Amen.

Let Jesus Show You the Way

"Come, follow me," Jesus said.
– Matthew 4:19

A Step at a Time

When living for Jesus and reaching out to people, sometimes it is best to take one step at a time. That way you have time to pray, hear God's answer, and then make the best choice possible.

Look at the pictures. There is a beginning picture and an ending picture. You get to draw the step that comes in the middle, between the beginning and the end. How fun!

Prayer

God, I want to do big things for you, but I guess I need to start with the little things. Show me the little things I can do to get started. Amen.

Let Jesus Show You the Way

"Come, follow me," Jesus said.
– Matthew 4:19

These Can Hurt

Match the words with what happened.

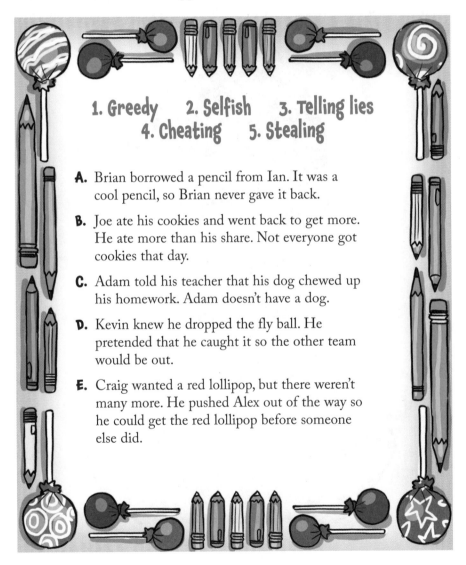

1. Greedy   2. Selfish   3. Telling lies
4. Cheating   5. Stealing

A. Brian borrowed a pencil from Ian. It was a cool pencil, so Brian never gave it back.

B. Joe ate his cookies and went back to get more. He ate more than his share. Not everyone got cookies that day.

C. Adam told his teacher that his dog chewed up his homework. Adam doesn't have a dog.

D. Kevin knew he dropped the fly ball. He pretended that he caught it so the other team would be out.

E. Craig wanted a red lollipop, but there weren't many more. He pushed Alex out of the way so he could get the red lollipop before someone else did.

Prayer

God, I always want to be honest with you. Help me see any hidden sins so I can ask for your forgiveness. Amen.

Let Jesus Show you the Way

"Come, follow me," Jesus said.
– Matthew 4:19

Some Things to Stay Away From

This boy has a button on his shirt. Write on the button an activity that you should avoid, such as stealing. Next to the boy write down more things you should avoid. How many did you name?

Prayer

God, show me the things and activities you want me to avoid. Help me follow you even if my friends do those things. Make me smart enough to know what might hurt me. Amen.

What Is Right?

I strive always to keep my conscience clear before God and man.
–Acts 24:16

Hard Lessons

"Ouch!" Zach yelled, jerking his finger back from the hot stove. "I burned myself. It really hurts."

"Run cold water over it," his mother said. "I'll get the burn cream." She returned and spread a thin coating on the tip of his finger. "Pain is a teacher," his mother said. "When you touch a hot stove, the pain tells you not to do it again. You'll be more careful the next time you're around the stove, right?"

"You bet I will," Zach said. He blew gently on his hurting finger.

"God lets you feel another kind of pain too," his mother said. "When you do something wrong, like telling a lie or taking something that doesn't belong to you, you feel bad on the inside. That bad feeling is the Holy Spirit reminding you not to do that thing again. Feeling pain inside is called your conscience."

"Sometimes God lets us feel bad so we'll do better next time?" Zach asked.

His mother nodded.

Your Turn

1. What lesson have you learned from physical pain?
2. What lesson have you learned from inside pain?

_____

_____

_____

_____

Prayer

God, it's hard to think that pain can be a good thing, but you know what you are doing. Thank you for making me the way I am. Amen.

What Is Right?

I strive always to keep my conscience clear before God and man.
–Acts 24:16

Taking Care of Your Body

God made you. He created every part of you, so he wants you to be healthy and do good things for your body. Put a checkmark in the box that shows how often you do these good things to take care of your body. You can add your own ideas to the chart too.

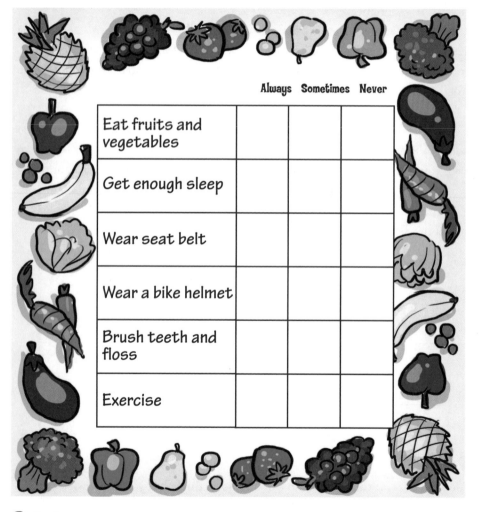

	Always	Sometimes	Never
Eat fruits and vegetables			
Get enough sleep			
Wear seat belt			
Wear a bike helmet			
Brush teeth and floss			
Exercise			

Prayer

God, I want to take good care of my body because that will please you. Help me learn more about staying healthy. Amen.

What Is Right?

I strive always to keep my conscience clear before God and man.
–Acts 24:16

Just Jesus and You

Draw a picture of you holding Jesus's hand or standing next to him. He is *always* with you. He will help you be strong and healthy. He will send you people and stories and more so you can learn how to take care of your mind, body, and heart. As you color Jesus and you, thank him for creating you.

Prayer

Jesus, no matter what I am doing, I know you are with me. I want to hold on to you so my faith will not get weak. Amen.

What Is Right?

I strive always to keep my conscience clear before God and man.
–Acts 24:16

God's Building Plans

"Do you know where God lives?" Mrs. Adams asked.

"Maybe God lives in church," Maria said.

"Excellent, Maria," Mrs. Adams said. "Jesus promised that whenever two or three Christians get together, he will be there."

Matt answered, "I think God lives everywhere."

Mrs. Adams nodded. "That's another good answer. No matter where we go, God is there."

Ian asked, "Does God live inside us?"

The Sunday-school teacher smiled. "Yes, Ian. Jesus said if we believe in him, he will come to live in us. A Christian's body is a temple for God's Holy Spirit. How well are you taking care of God's temple? Do you get enough sleep? Do you eat well? Are you getting exercise?"

"What about wearing seat belts in the car?" Matt said.

"Or putting on a helmet when I ride my bike," Maria added.

"How about brushing my teeth after meals?" Lucinda asked.

Mrs. Adams nodded. "When we take good care of ourselves, we're showing respect for God and his temple."

Your Turn

1. God created only one of you. How does that make you feel?
2. Since God lives in you, how are you taking care of yourself?

_____

_____

_____

_____

Prayer

Wow, God! You live in me? That is amazing. I'm going to be the best home I can be for you. Amen.

What Is Right?

I strive always to keep my conscience clear before God and man.
–Acts 24:16

Message Wheel

Unscramble the words in the parentheses below to find the hidden message:

Love (o d G) _ _ _
do (h a w t) _ _ _ _
is (o d o g) _ _ _ _

Prayer

God, I love you. Help me to do what is right. Thank you for creating me. Amen.

What Is Right?

I strive always to keep my conscience clear before God and man.
–Acts 24:16

Being Kind

God created you for a special purpose. He wants you to do good things and help people. Being kind is a great way to care for people. Are you kind every day?

— In the smallest circle, write something you can
   do to show kindness to your family.
— In the next circle, write some kindness you can do for someone at school.
— In the biggest circle, write some way you can be kind to nature.
   Remember, God created the plants, animals, earth, and sky too.

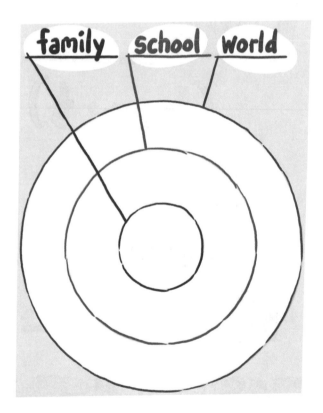

Prayer

God, you are the strongest one of all, and the Bible says you are love. I want to be strong in love too. Amen.

What Is Right?

I strive always to keep my conscience clear before God and man.
–Acts 24:16

Amazing You!

Unscramble the words that are in italics and write the correct word on the line.
When you are done, read these sentences about the totally amazing *you!*

God gave me *steo* _____
to help me walk.

God gave me *reas* _____
to listen.

God gave me *yees* _____
to see.

God gave me *dahns* _____
to work.

Prayer

God, thank you for the way my body works. You are an amazing Creator.
Amen.

People Are Good at Different Things

We have different gifts, according to the grace given to each of us.
– Romans 12:6

The Good Taster

"Mom," Danny asked, "why do you pick out Dad's clothes every morning? Isn't he old enough to choose his own shirt and pants?"

Mom laughed. "I help your dad find clothes that look good together. Your father is color blind. That means your dad can't see colors the way you do. Red and green look gray to him."

"Without you, Dad might dress up like a Christmas tree and never know it. A red sock on one foot and a green one on the other," Danny said.

"Your father has a wonderful sense of taste. He can take a sip of soup and know what it needs."

Danny knew his father was a chef at a fancy restaurant.

Mom said, "God doesn't give us all the same gifts."

"When we moved into this house," Danny remembered, "you picked out the new rugs and the paint for the walls."

"I'm good at colors," Mom agreed.

"Dad does the cooking in our house," Danny added, "because he is good at tasting things."

"What are you good at?" Mom asked, her eyes twinkling.

"I'm good at eating what Dad cooks!" Danny said with a grin.

Your Turn

1. Make a list of things you are good at.
2. Make a list for someone in your family. Are the lists the same?

_____

_____

_____

Prayer

God, I'm glad for the things I do well. They are gifts from you. Amen.

People Are Good at Different Things

We have different gifts, according to the grace given to each of us.
– Romans 12:6

Hey, God!

Finish these sentences with words or pictures to tell God what you are thankful for.

God, thank you for

_____.

God, thank you for

_____.

God, thank you for

_____.

God, thank you for

_____.

Prayer

God, sometimes I get down because I'm not good at something. But I know that doesn't matter to you because you made me just the way I am and you love me. I am thankful! Amen.

People Are Good at Different Things

We have different gifts, according to the grace given to each of us.
– Romans 12:6

Giving Gifts

At Christmastime it's fun to think about the gifts you will receive. But did you know you can give Jesus gifts every day of the year? Think of some gifts that you can give him.

Gift:
_____

Gift:
_____

Gift:
_____

Gift:
_____

Gift:
_____

Prayer

Jesus, I want to give you gifts every single day. The best gift I can give you is my life. Use me to help other people know you. Amen.

People Are Good at Different Things

We have different gifts, according to the grace given to each of us.
– Romans 12:6

Yay for You!

Johnny looked up. "Dad, how long is a mile?"

His father laid the newspaper on his lap. "It takes you fifteen minutes to walk to school, right? That's about a mile."

Johnny looked back at his book. "Wow! You know those tubes and hoses that carry blood through your body?"

"Blood vessels," his father said and grinned.

"Yeah," Johnny said. "That's what they are called. My schoolbook says I have 60,000 miles of those blood carriers in my body."

His father nodded. "That is is enough to go around the earth twice. You must be very special to God."

Johnny closed his book. "What do you mean?"

"Think about how well God made you," his father said. "Along with blood vessels, you have muscles, bones, skin, and a brain. Your body is better than any machine ever built."

Johnny looked at his hands and wiggled his fingers. "You're right!"

Your Turn

1. List some of your favorite things to do using your arms or legs.
2. List your favorite activities that require your ability to think.

_____

_____

_____

_____

Prayer

God, your Word says I am fearfully and wonderfully made. Even if I can't do some things, I am gifted in other things. Amen.

People Are Good at Different Things

We have different gifts, according to the grace given to each of us.
– Romans 12:6

All Good Gifts

God has given each of person special gifts. Gifts are everything you are good at. Your family and friends also have special gifts. Write the names of people you know next to the activities they are especially good at. Be sure to add yourself to the list.

Who do you know that is good at

reading? _____

playing sports? _____

listening? _____

speaking? _____

math? _____

teaching? _____

fishing? _____

music? _____

growing plants? _____

caring for animals? _____

Prayer

God, I am good at some things. I know these abilities are gifts from you. I know you have a purpose for me and my gifts. Help me understand what you want me to do. Amen.

People Are Good at Different Things

We have different gifts, according to the grace given to each of us.
– Romans 12:6

Like Samson, Like Me

One of God's gifts to Samson was the gift of great strength. In the space next to Samson, draw a picture of yourself using one of your gifts. How do you think God will use you?

Prayer

God, I want to give my whole self to you. Every bit of me. I can't wait to see what you will do through me. Amen.

People Are Good at Different Things

We have different gifts, according to the grace given to each of us.
– Romans 12:6

Handmade

Trace your hand on a piece of paper. Write or draw something on your paper hand that God wants you to do with your real hands.

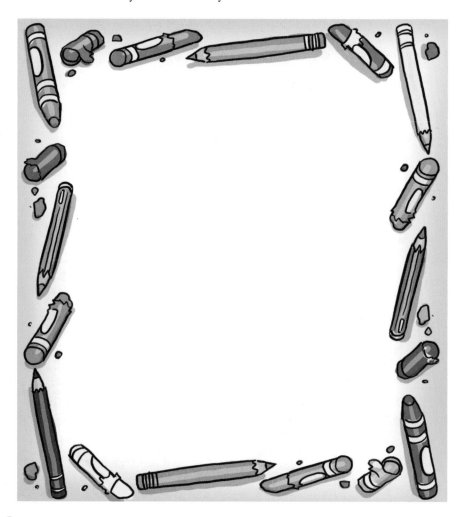

Prayer

God, no inventor in the world has ever made something as cool as my hand. I want to use both my hands to help others. Amen.

God Is Your Protector

Let the beloved of the LORD rest secure in him,
for he shields him all day long.
– Deuteronomy 33:12

God's Armor

Aaron missed the catch, and the basketball bounced off his head.

"Are you okay?" his father asked.

"Sure," Aaron said. He tapped his fist against the top of his head. "I have a hard head."

"It's a good thing," his dad said with a laugh. "Remember the time you conked your head with a hammer? And what about the jar of grape jelly that fell off the shelf and landed on your head?"

"That gave me a purple bruise over my eye," Aaron said.

"And didn't the Christmas tree fall on top of you once?"

"Sure. Ornaments broke," Aaron said, "but my head came through without a dent."

"Good thing God wrapped your brain in a skull," his dad said.

"What is a skull?" Aaron asked. "I see spooky pictures of skulls, but what is it really?"

"The skull is made of bone and covers your brain like armor," Dad explained. "It's like having a bicycle helmet inside your skin."

"I am glad God is watching out for my brain," Aaron said.

"God is watching out for your entire life," his dad said. "God has you wrapped in his protective arms."

Your Turn

1. Imagine God's arms wrapped around you. How does it make you feel?
2. What other ways does God protect you?

_____

_____

Prayer

God, I am going to be careful today, but I am not going to be afraid. I know you are taking care of me. Amen.

God Is Your Protector

Let the beloved of the LORD rest secure in him,
for he shields him all day long.

– Deuteronomy 33:12

God Is Your Shield

Write this week's verse, Deuteronomy 33:12, on the shield. Color and decorate your shield.

Prayer

God, I am thankful I don't have to be afraid because I know you are my shield all day long. Amen.

God Is Your Protector

Let the beloved of the LORD rest secure in him,
for he shields him all day long.
– Deuteronomy 33:12

The Same or Different?

God loves all of his children the same way. So when you meet someone who looks different, you can be sure God loves that person as much as he loves you. Draw faces, hair, and clothes on the two figures. Color the people so they resemble people you know. You can draw your teacher, doctor, minister, parent, bus driver, barber, coach, or store clerk. How are these people alike? How are these people different?

Prayer

God, people are like beautiful rainbows. I'm so glad you never run out of ideas for what people look and act like. Amen.

God Is Your Protector

Let the beloved of the LORD rest secure in him,
for he shields him all day long.
– Deuteronomy 33:12

Starting Small

Miguel watched his older brother, Jorge, lifting weights. Jorge put a long bar on a rack and added a round, metal weight to each end. When the weights were fastened in place, he raised the bar to his chest and then lowered it until it touched his legs. He did this ten times.

Breathing hard, Jorge set the bar down and wiped sweat from his face.

"I don't know how you can lift such a heavy weight," Miguel said.

"I couldn't at first," Jorge admitted. "When I started, I could only lift 60 pounds. So I did that over and over until I got stronger. Then I added more weight, just a little at a time. Soon I lifted 65 pounds. And then 70. I lifted that much until I could do more."

Miguel looked at the weights on the bar. "This is 120 pounds."

Jorge nodded. "And soon I'll be able to add another 10."

"When you started, was it hard?" Miguel asked.

"Sure," Jorge agreed. "My arms got sore. But things that matter come to us if we keep trying. It's called persevering."

Your Turn

1. What's the hardest thing you've ever learned to do?
2. Are you glad you didn't give up?

_____

_____

_____

_____

Prayer

Jesus, you asked God if you could quit, but you never did. You kept going all the way to the cross to die for me. Thank you. Amen.

God Is Your Protector

*Let the beloved of the L*ORD *rest secure in him,*
for he shields him all day long.

– Deuteronomy 33:12

Keep Going

The bike race is almost over, but the hardest part is just ahead. The bicycle racers have to get to the top of the hill and the finish line. They can't make any wrong turns or they won't finish the race. Will you help this racer get to the finish line? The race is hard. How would you encourage the bike rider when he gets tired?

Prayer

God, even when things seem tough or impossible, I know you are with me. Thank you for helping me reach my goals. Amen.

God Is Your Protector

Let the beloved of the LORD rest secure in him,
for he shields him all day long.
– Deuteronomy 33:12

God's Protection

Many things in nature will remind you that God protects all of his creation. What protection did God plan for these plants and animals? Draw their missing protective parts.

Turtle   Porcupine

Snail   Peanut

Prayer

God when I see things that have built-in protection to keep them safe, I can use it as a reminder to thank you for all you do for me to keep me safe. Amen.

God Is Your Protector

Let the beloved of the LORD rest secure in him,
for he shields him all day long.
– Deuteronomy 33:12

Controlling My Tongue

Have you discovered that sometimes it's hard to control what you say? Sometimes you say the wrong thing. Did you know that God can shield you from saying hurtful or mean things? He can!

Change these hurtful sentences into kinder sentences that won't hurt people's feelings.

"Why did you mess that up?"

"Get outta my way!"

"He's no good; we don't want him on our team."

Prayer

God, thank you for giving me a tongue to talk with. I hope my words will always please you. Amen.

God Is So Good to you

The LORD is my strength and my defense; he has become my salvation.
– Exodus 15:2

Saying Thank you

When the people of God found out that the Pharaoh of Egypt was setting them free, they gave thanks to God. They gathered in their homes for a special meal to honor God. They told stories about how good God is. They sang songs about his great power and love.

The next day, the Israelites gathered their belongings to leave Egypt. Some Egyptians gave them gifts so they would leave. God promised to lead his people to a land where there was plenty of everything.

After the Israelites left, the Pharaoh said, "What is this we have done, that we have let Israel go from serving us?" (Exodus 14:5). He led his army to get them back.

When the Israelites came to a wide sea, they were trapped and afraid.

Moses said, "Do not be afraid! Stand firm and you will see the deliverance the LORD will bring you today."

God sent a mighty wind and the sea rolled back. The Israelites walked across the sea floor without getting wet. When the Egyptian soldiers followed, God let the sea rush over them.

Do you know what God's people did? They worshipped God! They sang and danced on the shore of the sea.

Your Turn

1. What is a way you can say "thank you" to God?

_____

_____

_____

Prayer

God, if I worshipped you all day, every day, it would never be enough to show how much I love you. I praise your name! Amen.

God Is So Good to You

The LORD is my strength and my defense; he has become my salvation.
– Exodus 15:2

God, Your Helper

Moses wanted help, so God chose Moses's brother, Aaron, to assist him. Who has God chosen to help you? Draw a picture of a friend or family member who helps you. Tell that person, "Thank you!"

Prayer

God, will you help me remember to say "thanks" when somebody helps me? I know that is the right thing to do. Amen.

God Is So Good to You

The LORD is my strength and my defense; he has become my salvation.
– Exodus 15:2

You Are Growing

Are you growing stronger in the Lord every day? Trace the outline of your hand. On each finger, write or draw something that shows how you are growing into a person who pleases God.

Prayer

God, I want to please you. I am so glad that I keep getting stronger in you. Thank you for helping me grow. Amen.

God Is So Good to you

The LORD is my strength and my defense; he has become my salvation.
– Exodus 15:2

No Excuses

When Moses was young, his life was in danger, so he sneaked away to a place where he could live safely—in a land called Midian. He became a shepherd. Back in Egypt, life was hard for God's people. They were slaves and forced to work hard in the sun. The people prayed to God to save them, and he heard them.

One day while Moses was watching his family's sheep, he looked up in the hills and saw a bush that burned with strange fire. When Moses went closer, the voice of God came from the flames. God said, "Moses, I am sending you to Pharaoh to bring my people the Israelites out of Egypt" (Exodus 3:10).

Moses was afraid to go to Egypt because he was wanted for murder. He made excuses. He said he wasn't important. That he was a nobody. Why would the Pharaoh and the Israelites believe him?

"The elders of Israel will listen to you," God said. He told Moses, "I will stretch out my hand and strike the Egyptians with all the wonders I will perform… I will help you speak and will teach you what to say."

God said he would send Aaron too. "I will help both of you speak and will teach you what to do" (Exodus 4:14-15).

Moses decided to follow God's orders and go back to Egypt.

your Turn

1. Do you ask God for help?
2. What kind of help would you like from God today?

_____

_____

Prayer

God, there might be hard things and scary things in my future, but I know you will give me the help I need. Thank you for being with me. Amen.

God Is So Good to You

The LORD is my strength and my defense; he has become my salvation.
– Exodus 15:2

Sing to the LORD

Write a short poem or song to God. See if you can think of a tune to go with it. When you are done, sing your song or share your poem with your family and friends.

Prayer

Lord, I like to sing songs about you. I like to worship you. Thank you for being my salvation. Amen.

God Is So Good to You

The LORD is my strength and my defense; he has become my salvation.
– Exodus 15:2

Wise Up

God can do anything. He can save you with his mighty acts of judgment and protection. He can send people to give you his advice.

The pharaoh of Egypt found this out when Moses went to see him. But Pharaoh was a slow learner. It took him a long time to figure out that no one can fight God and win. When the Egyptian ruler didn't listen, God sent bad things that tormented the Egyptians. (You can read about this in Exodus 7–12.)

Can you help the Egyptian ruler? What message would you send him? Maybe "God Is Strong" or "God Always Wins." Think up your messages for the pharaoh and write them on the signs.

Prayer

God, there is nobody like you. When you step in, no one can stop you. Amen.

God Is So Good to You

The LORD is my strength and my defense; he has become my salvation.
– Exodus 15:2

Giving Thanks

Help the boy in the maze find his way home. Along the way, write the things he can be thankful for. (They might be the same things you are thankful for.)

Prayer

God, sometimes I feel lost. Even when life is hard, you are with me. I will worship you all the days of my life. I love you. Amen.

Live the Way God Wants

The people all responded together, "We will do everything the LORD has said."

– Exodus 19:8

Living Right

When Moses led the people out of their slavery in Egypt, God knew he needed to teach his people how to be his children. If his people would follow his teachings, they would be happy and blessed (Exodus 19–20).

God called Moses to climb to the top of Mount Sinai, the very same mountain where he had seen the burning bush. When Moses got to the top, God came down to be with him. The people at the base of the mountain were afraid because they saw smoke and fire on top of the mountain. They heard God's voice, and it sounded like thunder.

God basically said, "Moses, I will give you 10 laws to carry to my people. These laws will show them what pleases me. If they keep these laws, they love and honor me." God wrote the 10 laws on solid rock. (Today many people call these the Ten Commandments.) Moses took the two stone tablets down the mountain.

God cares how you live. He wants you to follow and obey him because you are his child.

Your Turn

1. If you didn't know God's rules, would you know how to please him?
2. Write down as many of the Ten Commandments you know without looking them up.

_____

_____

_____

_____

Prayer

God, help me learn what pleases you. That's what I want to do. Amen.

Live the Way God Wants

The people all responded together, "We will do everything the LORD has said."

– Exodus 19:8

Learning God's Laws

Here are the 10 laws God gave to Moses. Someone forgot to put in the "Os." Change the "I" to "in" and remove the apostrophe after "O" both times. If there are laws you do not understand, ask an adult to explain to you. If you want to read more about these laws, you can find them in your Bible in Exodus 20.

1. D____ n____t w____rship any g____d except me.

2. D____ n____t make id____ls.

3. D____ n____t misuse my name.

4. Remember that the Sabbath Day bel____ngs to me. N____ ____ne

   is t____ w____rk ____n that day.

5. Respect y____ur father and y____ur m____ther.

6. D____ n____t murder.

7. Be faithful in marriage.

8. D____ n____t steal.

9. D____ n____t tell lies ab____ut

   ____thers.

10. D____ n____t want anything that

    bel____ngs to s____me ____ne else.

Prayer

God, thank you for your laws. They help me know how to please and obey you. Amen.

Live the Way God Wants

The people all responded together, "We will do everything the LORD has said."

– Exodus 19:8

House Rules

Are there rules at your house that your parents expect you to obey? List five of them.

1. _____

2. _____

3. _____

4. _____

5. _____

Prayer

Lord, I want to follow the rules in my home, but sometimes I make mistakes and disobey. When I do, I will apologize to you and to my parents. I'll ask for forgiveness. I'm so glad you love me. Amen.

Live the Way God Wants

The people all responded together, "We will do everything the LORD has said."

– Exodus 19:8

Doing or Talking?

Jesus told a story about what we do and say (Matthew 21:28-32). The following story is very similar.

A farmer had a tree stump in the middle of his wheat field. So he went to his two sons to ask for help. Their names were Sam and Hank. Both were big and strong.

The farmer said, "That old tree stump is in my way. Will you dig it out for me?"

Sam said, "No problem, Dad. I'll get rid of the stump for you. Just leave it to me."

Hank said, "I'm too busy, Dad. I can't do it."

The farmer waited and waited for Sam to do the job.

Hank was sorry he had said no to his father. One morning, Hank took a shovel and an ax to the field. He spent all day digging the stump out.

The farmer saw Hank coming home that evening tired, sweaty, and dirty. The farmer saw Sam sitting in an easy chair reading. The father looked into the field and smiled to see that the stump was gone.

Your Turn

1. Who do you think pleased his father more? Why?
2. When you're asked to help, do you hurry to obey or do you wait? Which is better?

_____

_____

_____

Prayer

God, it's easy to say, "Sure, I'll follow you." I also need to do what you want me to do. Amen.

Live the Way God Wants

The people all responded together, "We will do everything the LORD has said."

– Exodus 19:8

That's Not How the Story Goes

These sentences retell the story of the father, his two sons, and the stump you read yesterday. However, there are some mistakes. The numbers tell you how many incorrect words there are in each sentence. Circle the words that don't belong and write in the correct words.

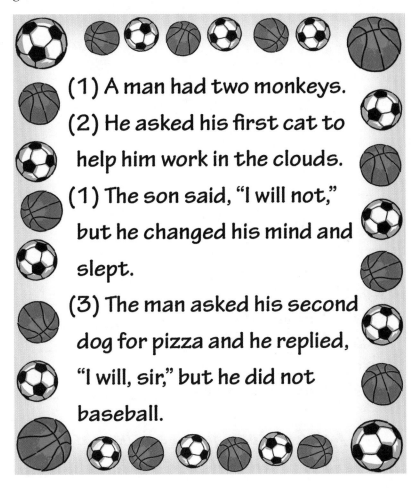

(1) A man had two monkeys.

(2) He asked his first cat to help him work in the clouds.

(1) The son said, "I will not," but he changed his mind and slept.

(3) The man asked his second dog for pizza and he replied, "I will, sir," but he did not baseball.

Prayer

God, I want to do the things I say I'll do. I want to do what you want me to do too. That's part of what being a Christian is about. Amen.

Live the Way God Wants

The people all responded together, "We will do everything the LORD has said."

– Exodus 19:8

Jobs for You

In each circle draw or write one job that can be done by someone your age. Then answer the questions.

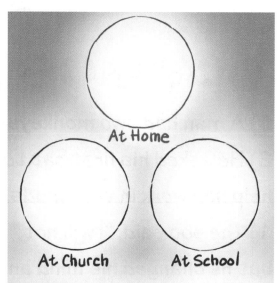

At Home

At Church   At School

Is there a job you are scared to try?
What job is it?_____
What job do you like?_____
What job do you dislike?_____
  Why?_____
What job do you want to try?_____

*Ask God to help you do the jobs
He wants you to do.*

Prayer

Dear God, please help me to do the jobs you want me to do. Amen.

Live the Way God Wants

The people all responded together, "We will do everything the Lord has said."

– Exodus 19:8

How Many Gods?

Some people think there are many gods who watch over us. What do you think? If you solve the puzzle, you will know what the Bible says about this. Cross out every 2, 3, and 4. When you finish, read the message that is left.

Prayer

God, I know there is no one else like you. You are one of a kind. I will only worship you. Amen.

God Cares About the Little Things

Even the very hairs of your head are all numbered.
– Matthew 10:30

Even Your Hair

Elisha was a prophet of God. He usually showed God's power by asking for miracles.

One time, Elisha's friends were cooking stew. One of the friends chopped some gourds up and dumped the pieces into the stew pot. Someone yelled, "There is death in the pot!" The stew was ruined because the gourds were poisonous. Elisha asked God to clean the poison out. Elisha threw a little flour into the stew and said, "Serve it to the people" (2 Kings 4:41). The poison was gone! They ate and gave thanks to God.

Another time, Elisha's friend was cutting trees. The iron head came off the ax handle and splashed into the river. "Oh no, my Lord!" the man said. "It was borrowed!"

Elisha asked, "Where did it fall?" Then he threw a stick into the river and prayed for God to help. The heavy ax head floated to the top of the water, and the man was able to get it out (2 Kings 6:5).

Saving a pot of stew and finding a lost ax head are little things. Maybe Elisha did things like this to remind people that God cares about the little things too. God cares about everything you care about.

Your Turn

1. Is it okay to ask God about little things like a lost toy?
2. What little thing do you want to pray about right now?

_____

_____

_____

Prayer

God, thank you for caring about the little stuff that happens to me. Amen.

God Cares About the Little Things

Even the very hairs of your head are all numbered.
– Matthew 10:30

Watching Over the Birds

A sparrow is a small bird. Jesus said that God watches over the sparrows. God knows every time a sparrow lands or falls. If God is so careful to watch over tiny birds, you know He will watch over the small things in your life.

How many birds can you add to this picture? Draw some flying and some on the branches. Draw some on the ground. Put some baby birds in nests. No matter how many you draw, God will be able to watch them all.

Prayer

God, I know there will never be too many things for you to watch over. Thank you that you care about everything in my life. Amen.

God Cares About the Little Things

Even the very hairs of your head are all numbered.
– Matthew 10:30

Made for Each Other

God knows everyone needs help sometimes. What a lonely world it would be if we didn't have friends and helpers. Here are pictures of things two people can do together. Draw the second person in each picture.

Prayer

God, thank you for knowing when to send people to help me. I'm glad I have family and friends! Amen.

God Cares About the Little Things

Even the very hairs of your head are all numbered.
– Matthew 10:30

Trusting God

When Moses led God's people out of Egypt, it was a long walk to the land God was giving them. They had to slog through miles of hot desert sand. They were afraid they would not find food or water.

Moses told them not to be afraid because God would take care of them. "You are his children. He will give you what you need. Trust him."

One morning when the people woke up and came out of their tents, they saw white flakes on the rocks, plants, and ground. "What is it?" they asked. They picked up the tiny flakes.

"It is the bread the LORD has given you to eat," Moses said. The people of Israel called the bread manna (Exodus 16:31). Moses said to gather only what they needed for that day. God promised to keep sending manna until they reached the promised land.

This was how God taught the people to trust him to take care of them day after day. There was no need to be afraid of tomorrow.

When tomorrow comes, God will still be taking care of you too.

Your Turn

1. Does worrying about tomorrow make things better or worse? Why?
2. When you worry, what can you do to not be afraid?

_____

_____

_____

_____

Prayer

God, I trust you to take care of me today and tomorrow. Amen.

God Cares About the Little Things

Even the very hairs of your head are all numbered.
– Matthew 10:30

God Helps Moses

Remember the story about God sending manna to feed his people in the desert? Mark out the picture that doesn't belong in that story. (Reread yesterday's story if you need help remembering.) Put numbers in the small boxes next to each picture to show the right order of the story.

God gave the people food each day. It was called manna.

The people were having a big party because they had been set free.

Moses and the people of Israel walked a long time in the desert.

God told the people to take just what they needed to eat in one day.

Prayer

God, because you know me, I can trust you to give me what I need each day, just like you did for the people of Israel. Amen.

God Cares About the Little Things

Even the very hairs of your head are all numbered.
– Matthew 10:30

Differences

Look at these two boys. Find at least five differences in the way they look and the way they dress. Can you find even more?

Prayer

God, when I go someplace new, I am a stranger. People don't know me. But no matter where I go, you are always with me. I never have to feel alone. Thank you. Amen.

God Cares About the Little Things

Even the very hairs of your head are all numbered.
– Matthew 10:30

Family Portrait

The Bible tells you that Jesus knows you, even down to the number of hairs on your head. You don't know how many hairs are on your head, but you do know your family. Draw a picture of them in the house and color them.

Did Jesus have brothers and sisters? Did he have friends? In your Bible, look up these verses. What do they tell you about Jesus?

John 2:2, Matthew 12:46, Mark 3:31, Mark 6:3, Luke 8:19-20

_____

_____

Prayer

Jesus, I want to know all the facts I can about hou. Thank hou for knowing all the facts about me. I will read my Bible so I will learn more about hou. Amen.

You Are Special to God

God has surely listened and has heard my prayer.
– Psalm 66:19

Made to Be Amazing

Did you know that a lot of animals hear better than you? If you have a dog, you know he hears things you don't. When someone comes to your door, your dog knows before you do.

Have you seen robins in your yard looking for worms? Robins can hear them crawling underground. By listening, the robin knows where to grab a worm. Have you tried listening to a worm digging in the dirt? You probably couldn't hear it.

The fennec fox lives in Africa and has big ears. It hunts in the desert at night. His ears help him hear when there is danger. He can also hear the little animals he hopes to eat.

Have you ever said a prayer and wondered if God heard you? Maybe you whispered the prayer while lying in bed. Maybe you didn't even say the prayer out loud but just in your head. It doesn't matter because God hears every prayer. Whether you think it or shout it, God hears you. Whether you are alone in a quiet room or in the middle of a noisy crowd, God hears you. Whether you are on the top of a mountain or deep in a cave underground, God hears your prayer. You can talk to God anytime and know he hears every thought and word.

Your Turn

1. How often do you talk to God?
2. How do you feel when you talk to God?

_____

_____

_____

_____

Prayer

God, some people might think my prayers are dumb, but not you. You listen to every word. Thank you for being the best listener of all. Amen.

You Are Special to God

God has surely listened and heard my voice in prayer.
– Psalm 66:19

Ears to Hear

Draw the correct ears on the animals and person.

Prayer

Lord, thank you for my ears. Also, thank you for hearing all my prayers even when I don't say them out loud. Amen.

You Are Special to God

God has surely listened and heard my voice in prayer.
– Psalm 66:19

You Cannot Hide from God

Wherever you go, God will find you. Can you can find the seven boys hidden in this picture?

Prayer

God, thank you for listening to my prayers no matter where I am. Amen.

You Are Special to God

God has surely listened and heard my voice in prayer.
– Psalm 66:19

Always Watching

Can you guess what animal has the biggest eyes in the world? Here's a clue. The animal lives in the deep ocean where it is very dark.

Here's another clue. This animal has many arms like an octopus.

Give up?

The animal with the biggest eyes in the world is the giant squid. Its eyes are the size of basketballs and bigger than your head. Those eyes help the squid find its way in the dark.

Do you think God can see as well as a giant squid? Absolutely! In fact, God sees everything everywhere all the time. Nothing is too far away or too small. Nothing is too dark. Nothing can hide you from God.

God always keeps an eye on you. Even if you get lost from your parents, you can never get lost from God. When you are in trouble, God sees what is going on. When you are afraid, God sees your problem. When you are hurting, God sees into your heart.

Maybe the giant squid has amazing eyes, but God's vision is even more awesome. He watches over you and all his children.

Your Turn

1. Do you have a favorite hiding place? Can God see you there?
2. Why is God always watching you?

_____

_____

_____

_____

Prayer

God, I'm so glad you can see me all the time. I feel safe knowing you are watching over me and listening when I talk to you. Amen.

You Are Special to God

God has surely listened and heard my voice in prayer.
– Psalm 66:19

Listen to the Radio

Do you like listening to music? Write a prayer in the music player. Now read the prayer out loud to God.

Prayer

God, when I remember to pray, I feel closer to you. No matter where I am or what I'm doing, I know you always hear me. Thank you! Amen.

You Are Special to God

God has surely listened and heard my voice in prayer.
– Psalm 66:19

The LORD's Prayer

Look up "the Lord's Prayer" in your Bible, in Matthew 6:9-13. Fill in the blanks and then read it out loud. If you don't understand any words, ask an adult to explain them to you.

Our Father in _____,

hallowed be your name.

Your kingdom _____, your will be

_____ on _____ as it is in

_____. Give us today our daily

_____. And forgive us our debts, as

we also have _____ our debtors. And

lead us not into _____,

but deliver us from the evil one. Amen.

You Are Special to God

God has surely listened and heard my voice in prayer.
– Psalm 66:19

Prayer Journal

For the next week, pray about something important to you each day. Record what you prayed about on this prayer journal page. Keep praying about these things until God gives you an answer. When he answers your prayer, come back to this page and write what God said and the date he said it. Remember, sometimes God answers "no" or "not right now."

Prayer

God, I will keep praying about something until you answer. Your answer might be "yes" or "no" or "not now." No matter what the answer is, I know you want only the best for me. Amen.

God Is the Highest of All

The LORD Most High is awesome, the great King over all the earth.
– Psalm 47:2

Above the Stars

Have you ever watched birds and wondered how high they can fly? The champion high flyer is an African bird called a griffon vulture. We know the griffon vulture can fly very high because an airplane ran into one seven miles above the ground. Most birds can't fly so high because the air gets thinner the higher you go. At seven miles above the earth you would not be able to breathe. That's why jet pilots wear oxygen masks.

The griffon vulture has large wings that helps it fly way up in the thin air. The griffon looks down on bluebirds, robins, and eagles.

Seven miles is high, but God is higher. One name for God is "God the Most High." That means God is the best in every way.

God is most high in wisdom. Nobody knows as much as God. Nobody understands as much as God. God is most high in goodness. Everything he does is right. He never does anything sinful. He never makes mistakes. God is most high in power. Nobody is as strong and mighty as God. God is most high in love. Nobody can outdo God in caring, loving, kindness, and mercy.

Your Turn

1. What three words describe how you feel knowing the Most High God watches over you?
2. Would you like to fly as high as a griffon vulture? Why or why not?

_____

_____

_____

_____

Prayer

God, nothing is as important to me as you are. Amen.

God Is the Highest of All

The Lord Most High is awesome, the great King over all the earth.
– Psalm 47:2

Nothing to Be Afraid Of

As long as you are in the arms of Jesus, nothing can grab you or carry you away. Draw another monster that bothers you in this picture. You are safe with Jesus. If you want, you can give your monster a name that describes it.

Prayer

God, when I start to worry or get scared, help me to remember to pray and ask for your help. You are always with me, so I don't have to be afraid. Amen.

God Is the Highest of All

The Lord Most High is awesome, the great King over all the earth.
– Psalm 47:2

Numero Uno

Sometimes we give awards to people who are good at spelling or who play soccer well. Maybe we should give God an award for being the best at everything! Of course, God doesn't need an award, but it's fun to tell God how great he is.

Use your imagination and your markers or crayons to finish this award for God. You can use words or pictures. How will you show that God is the highest and best?

Prayer

God, you deserve every award! The best award I can give you is my heart. I freely give my heart to you because you are my Lord and Savior. Amen.

God Is the Highest of All

The Lord Most High is awesome, the great King over all the earth.
– Psalm 47:2

In God's Arms

Many animals can hold on to things very tightly. The snapping turtle has powerful jaws. If you can get a snapping turtle to bite a stick, you can pick up the stick and carry the turtle around. He will not let go! Just make sure he bites the stick and not your finger!

Birds have feet made for holding on. Have you ever wondered how birds sleep? When a bird is on a branch, its feet will hold on even if it falls asleep. The bird has feet that lock into place.

The barnacle is a little ocean animal that glues its shell to rocks, to the bottoms of ships, and even to whales. Barnacle glue is hard and strong. If you tried to pry a barnacle from a rock with a pocketknife, you would snap the blade.

God is even better at holding on. You can't see God's hand, and you can't feel God's arms around you, but you have God's promise that he will never let you go. What can take you away from God? Bad grades? Getting sick? Family trouble? Bullies? No! Nothing can pull you out of God's loving arms. Even when you die, God still holds you as you enter his heavenly kingdom.

Your Turn

1. Why do you think God holds you so tightly?
2. How does it make you feel to know that God is holding you?

_____

_____

_____

_____

Prayer

God, I am always safe and snug in your hands. I trust you. Amen.

God Is the Highest of All

The LORD Most High is awesome, the great King over all the earth.
– Psalm 47:2

God Is King over All the Earth!

God is the Lord Most High, the great King over all the earth. Even though you don't know what God really looks like, draw how you picture him in your mind. Have Him sit in the throne on top of the earth.

Prayer

Dear God, when I think of you sitting on your throne in heaven, I know I am in good hands. You are awesome. I am so glad I am one of your children. Amen.

God Is the Highest of All

The LORD Most High is awesome, the great King over all the earth.
– Psalm 47:2

Who Are You?

God already knows everything about you. He also wants you to know him as well as you know your family. God gives you clues about who he is in the Bible. Isaiah 42:8 says, "I am the LORD, that is my name."

Write the names of your family and friends on the magnifying glass. Give clues for each person that would tell others about them. Pray for each person.

Prayer

God, teach me to give others clues about who you are. I want everybody I know to love you and know you. Amen.

God Is the Highest of All

The LORD Most High is awesome, the great King over all the earth.
– Psalm 47:2

My Store

Psalm 124:8 tells you that "your help is in the name of the LORD." That is why God wants you to know his name.

The sign in front of a store tells the name of the store and usually something about the store. Write your own store name on the sign on the front of the store. Put your name on the store window. God loves your name!

'

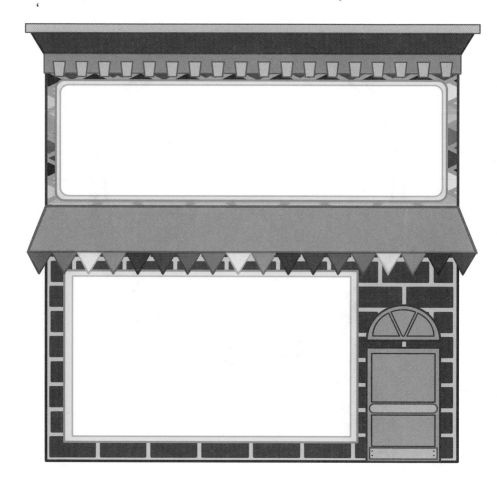

Prayer

God, thank you that you know my name. Teach me more about your name. I want to tell others about you. Amen.

God Never Changes

Jesus Christ is the same yesterday and today and forever.
– Hebrews 13:8

Already Perfect

Some animals change colors with the seasons. The goldfinch is a bright-yellow bird in the summer. It has drab brown feathers in the winter. Some rabbits are brown in the summer and turn white in the winter so they can hide in the snow. The chameleon changes color whenever it wants to. If a chameleon rides in your red wagon, it will turn red. If it climbs next to a mustard bottle, the lizard will turn yellow. You can probably guess what happens if a chameleon jumps on your blue jeans.

Many things change, but God never does. He loves you today, and he will love you tomorrow. God has always been holy and good, and he will always be holy and good. God was forgiving yesterday, and he will be forgiving 100,000 years from now.

People change because they need to grow. That is one kind of changing. Some things about all people need to be better. We are not perfect, so we want to keep on changing and becoming more like God wants us to be.

Your Turn

1. God never changes. Does anything else never change?
2. What would you like to change about yourself?

_____

_____

_____

_____

Prayer

Jesus, I know you never change, but I'm changing all the time. Help me change in ways that make me more like you. Amen.

God Never Changes

Jesus Christ is the same yesterday and today and forever.
– Hebrews 13:8

Your Timeline

Add dates to the timeline to show changes in your life. You may have to ask your mom or dad for help. Add some things you have done and things you think you will do.

   Remember, God was with you when you were born. God is with you now. And God will be with you for your entire life and beyond.

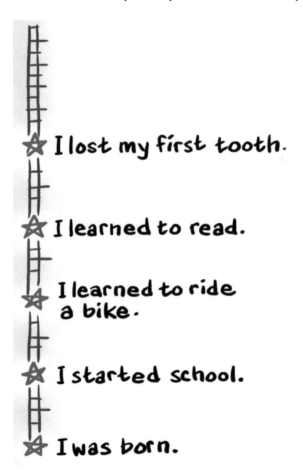

I lost my first tooth.

I learned to read.

I learned to ride a bike.

I started school.

I was born.

Prayer

Jesus, even though things change in my life, you never do. This makes me feel safe. Amen.

God Never Changes

Jesus Christ is the same yesterday and today and forever.
– Hebrews 13:8

Grow and Change!

Match the pictures to show how some things change.

Prayer

God, thank you that you never change. Knowing that you are the same yesterday and today and forever makes me feel secure. I know that I can always count on you. Amen.

God Never Changes

Jesus Christ is the same yesterday and today and forever.
– Hebrews 13:8

The Oldest

Some people live to be very old. Maybe you know someone who is 100 years old. Can you imagine a birthday cake with 100 candles burning on top? Someone should have a bucket of water nearby just in case.

Even though 100 years is a long time for a person to live, some animals live longer than that. Macaw parrots might live to be over 100 years old. Some tortoises live 150 to 200 years. The arctic whale can live more than 200 years. The quahog, a simple shellfish, might even live 400 years.

None of this seems very long compared to God. How old is God? There is no way to answer that because God has always been. There was a time before you got here, and a time before your parents got here, but there was never a time before God. God is older than the oldest thing in the world. God will always be here. He will never go away.

Your bicycle will get rusty someday, and you'll need a new one. Your favorite shoes will wear out, and you'll get a new pair. Sooner or later the pages will fall out of this book, and you will have to get another one. But you will never need a new God, not even if you live to be 100 years old.

Your Turn

1. How old is the oldest person you know?
2. How does it feel to know you will live with God forever?

_____

_____

_____

_____

Prayer

God, you have been around so long I can't even imagine it. After the mountains are worn out, you will still be my God! Amen.

God Never Changes

Jesus Christ is the same yesterday and today and forever.
– Hebrews 13:8

God's Comfort

You can count on God to never change. He will always be there for you. You can trust him to care for you. God gives you people who will take care of you and remind you how much God loves you. Who are the people who remind you that God is taking care of you?

Draw a picture of one of them. Write down some of the ways that person brings you the message of God's love.

Prayer

God, I know you will always be with me and that I can trust you with my life. Thank you for bringing people into my life who take care of me. They remind me of how much you love me and take care of me. Amen.

God Never Changes

Jesus Christ is the same yesterday and today and forever.
– Hebrews 13:8

God Never Moves

You can count on God to never change. As you go through life, you will be changing all the time. Decide today that the choices you make will draw you closer to God.

Find the correct path in the maze to get to Jesus. He's waiting for you!

Prayer

God, you are perfect and you never change. I want to always grow more like you. Help me make choices that bring me closer to you. Amen.

God Never Changes

Jesus Christ is the same yesterday and today and forever.
– Hebrews 13:8

Jesus Never Changes

God has an important message for you! Unscramble the words to find out what it is.

sJuse tshCir is het msea dryeetyas and odyta and reofervr.

Prayer

God, I know that many things change, but you never do. I am thankful that you love me always. Amen.

God Brings You Closer

Come near to God and he will come near to you.
– James 4:8

Stickers and Stinkers

Some animals are not friendly. If you made a list of animals you wouldn't want to meet face-to-face, one might be the porcupine. Although a porcupine isn't mean, it isn't friendly, either. A porcupine is covered with stickers called quills. If you touch a porcupine, the quills will stab your hand. They have barbs on the end, so they are not easy to pull out. If you meet a porcupine, don't pet it! Porcupines want to be left alone. Hug a porcupine? Forget it.

Skunks are even less friendly than porcupines. At least you can get close to a porcupine. Don't try that with a skunk. Keep your distance from the little black-and-white animal. The skunk has a special squirter under his tail that shoots a stream of stinky juice. Skunk juice odor is the worst. If a skunk sprays you, you'll have to throw your clothes in the garbage. Even after a couple of baths, you will smell bad for days. When a skunk raises his tail, he is telling you, "Stay away from me."

Aren't you glad God is not like the porcupine or the skunk? God is just the opposite. Jesus says, "Come to me!" He says, "Let the tired come to me." Jesus says, "Let the thirsty come to me." He says, "Let the children come to me." God never pushes you away. He loves you and always wants you to come closer to him.

Your Turn

1. Is God friendly? Why do you think that?
2. What does God's friendliness mean to you?

_____

_____

Prayer

God, some people might not want me around, but you are always my friend. Amen.

God Brings You Closer

Come near to God and he will come near to you.
– James 4:8

A Faithful Friend

A faithful friend sticks with you even when it's not fun. Do you have a friend who sticks with you even when you are angry, or hurt, or in a bad mood? Write a thank You to God for your faithful friends. Also thank God for always being your faithful friend.

Dear God, Thank You for

_____

who is a good friend
and is faithful to me. Thank You
for always being
my Friend and Protector
Amen.

Prayer

Dear God, thank you that I can always count on you. Please help me to be a faithful person. Amen.

God Brings You Closer

Come near to God and he will come near to you.
– James 4:8

Pal or Porcupine?

God wants you to stay close to him. He also wants you to stay close to your family and friends. Are you a good friend? Do people enjoy hanging with you? Do you have any "porcupine" habits?

Help the boy turn from a porcupine to a pal. Cross out the things that push people away. Circle the things that help people stay close to each other. You can add to the list other things that make a good friend.

FORGIVE   FRIENDLY
ANGRY   INSULTS
BLAME   FROWN
SMILE
FUN
YELL
STINGY
KIND   SHARE
PUT DOWNS   LISTENER

Prayer

God, please help me be a good friend. Amen.

God Brings You Closer

Come near to God and he will come near to you.
– James 4:8

Higher Than You Can Count

Over 100 years ago, a man named John had a dog named Bobby. John was a policeman. He and Bobby often walked the streets of their town together late at night. When John died, he was buried at the Greyfriars Church. Even though his master was gone, Bobby never forgot him. Every day the little terrier went to sit on the grave of his old friend. The dog spent so much time at Greyfriars Church that people began to call him Greyfriars Bobby.

How long do you think Greyfriars Bobby stayed by his master's grave? A month? A year? Ten years? The loving dog spent fourteen years remembering his master. Greyfriars Bobby stayed beside the grave until the day he died. He was buried not far away from his master. The people of the town loved Bobby. They put up a statue of the faithful dog. Bobby's face is even carved on the church organ.

Bobby was awesome, but God is even more amazing. Bobby was faithful to his friend for years, but you can't count the years of God's faithfulness. God never dies, and God's love never stops. He will stay beside you forever.

Your Turn

1. Think of the faithful people in your life. How does their love help you understand God's love? Explain.
2. How does your love help them understand God's love?

_____

_____

_____

Prayer

God, is it okay for a dog to remind me of how faithful You are? Bobby was faithful his whole life. You will be faithful forever. Amen.

God Brings you Closer

Come near to God and he will come near to you.
– James 4:8

God Has the Whole World in His Hands

Can you find where you live on the globe? Draw a star at that spot. Let this picture remind you that God is taking care of people all over the world. Even though the world is large, God is near to all of his children.

Do you know the words to "He's Got the Whole World in His Hands"? If you do, sing it.

Prayer

God, when I think of all the people in the world, I am amazed you are with me—and with everyone who loves you, no matter where we live. You are an awesome God! Amen.

God Brings You Closer

Come near to God and he will come near to you.
– James 4:8

God Is Near

Circle these words in the word search: GOD, JESUS, FRIEND, FAITHFUL

Prayer

God, when I think of all the people you love, I know that I can trust you for everything. No one is as powerful and faithful as you are. You are perfect. Amen.

God Brings You Closer

Come near to God and he will come near to you.
– James 4:8

Some Favorite Things

Did you know you are one of God's favorite people? He loves you and died for you so that you can live for eternity in heaven with him.

Make a list of some of your favorite things. Don't forget to include people you love!

My Favorite Things

_____
_____
_____
_____
_____
_____
_____
_____
_____

Prayer

Dear God, thank you for loving me. When I think about spending eternity with you, I am glad. I never want to be away from you. Amen.

God Has a Home Waiting for You

We have a building from God, an eternal house in heaven, not built by human hands.
– 2 Corinthians 5:1

When Things Change

Nathan looked through the car window as his dad drove along a quiet street. On either side of the road, Nathan saw half-built houses. Dad stopped the car. "This is it," he said.

Everyone got out of the car. Nathan looked around in confusion. "There's nothing here," he said. "Just this field with tall grass."

"That's where our new house is going to be," Dad said. "This is where your bedroom will be, Nathan. The family room will be over there," Dad said, pointing toward a small bush. He walked a few yards. "Girls, you'll sleep here."

"What do you think, Nathan?" Mom asked.

Nathan shrugged. "I still don't see why we need to move."

"We need a bigger house," Mom said. "Your grandmother is going to move in with us, and we need more space."

"But I'll miss the old house," Nathan said.

Grandma put an arm around Nathan's shoulder. "I'm sad to leave my old house too," she said. "But we don't get to stay in one place forever, at least not until we get to heaven. Nothing in this world lasts forever, not houses or people."

"I see," Nathan said. "Where is your room going to be?"

She pointed to a maple tree. "My window will look out on that tree," she said, "so I can keep an eye on you in your tree house."

"Tree house?" Nathan said. "Wow! This is going to be great."

Your Turn

1. New things can make us feel overwhelmed. What is something you can do when you feel overwhelmed?

Prayer

God, things don't always stay the same, but I know you will take care of me through every change. Thank you. Amen.

God Has a Home Waiting for You

We have a building from God, an eternal house in heaven, not built by human hands.
– 2 Corinthians 5:1

Your Stuff

In the moving truck, draw a picture of three things you own that you really like. Thank God for letting you have those items to enjoy.

Prayer

God, I am thankful for the things I have. But I am thankful that you are my Savior even more. Amen.

God Has a Home Waiting for You

We have a building from God, an eternal house in heaven, not built by human hands.
– 2 Corinthians 5:1

New Things

Put a checkmark by the new things you had to get used to. Choose the one that was hardest for you, and write it into the prayer.

_____ New school

_____ New teacher

_____ New brother or sister

_____ New coach

_____ New house

_____ New doctor

_____ New mother or father

Prayer

God, thank you for helping me when things change.

Please help me get used to my new

_____.

Amen.

God Has a Home Waiting for you

We have a building from God, an eternal house in heaven, not built by human hands.
– 2 Corinthians 5:1

Where Is your Heart?

It was moving day at last. For months, Nathan's family had waited for the carpenters to finish building their new house. Nathan watched as the movers loaded furniture, mattresses, and boxes into a big truck. Finally the men carried the last box out and closed the big truck door.

Nathan's mom, sisters, and grandma were already at the new house.

Nathan's dad put an arm around him as the truck drove away.

"Does it make you scared?" Nathan asked. "All our stuff is on that truck. If that truck crashes, we'll lose everything."

"We would still have our family," Dad said.

"Yeah, but you know what I mean," Nathan said.

"Sure, I know what you mean," Dad said. "It would make me sad to lose my things. But things are just things. Wherever your treasure is, that's where your heart will be. Jesus said so. Our hearts are with whatever we love the most."

"I love Jesus the most," Nathan said, "and my family next. But I still hope our stuff gets to the new house okay."

Dad hugged Nathan. "Me too!"

your Turn

1. Is it wrong to love things as much as people? Why?
2. Why do you love God most of all?

_____

_____

_____

Prayer

God, thank you for the cool stuff I have, but thanks even more for being my God. You are the best! Amen.

God Has a Home Waiting for You

We have a building from God, an eternal house in heaven, not built by human hands.
– 2 Corinthians 5:1

A Good Foundation

Just like a house needs a good foundation, we do too. Color the words that show Jesus is your foundation. Some of the words will be left out because they are not part of our good foundation.

Prayer

God, thank you that you are my firm foundation. You are the one I can count on because you are always with me. Amen.

God Has a Home Waiting for You

We have a building from God, an eternal house in heaven, not built by human hands.
– 2 Corinthians 5:1

Strong Walls

Just like a house needs strong walls, you need Jesus to help you be strong. When do you need to ask him to help you to be strong? Read the words on the rock-climbing wall. Add your own reason for needing help from God at the top of the wall.

Prayer

Fill me with Jesus" to "fill me with your Spirit" or "please help me be strong for you. Amen.

God Has a Home Waiting for You

We have a building from God, an eternal house in heaven, not built by human hands.
– 2 Corinthians 5:1

God, Our Helper

Bricks make a strong foundation. Unscramble the words on the bricks, and write the correct spelling on the bottom bricks. Each word is about God. Circle the words that remind you that God will take care of you when bad things happen.

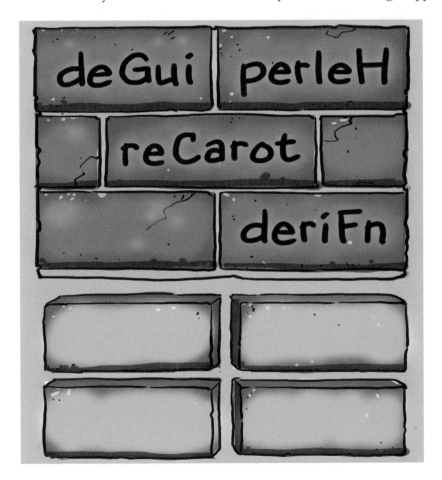

Prayer

God, I don't want bad things to come, but when they do I know you will help me handle it. Amen.

Being a Christian Means Following Jesus

Since we live by the Spirit, let us keep in step with the Spirit.
– Galatians 5:25

Thin Ice

"Come on, Alex!" Manny yelled. "Follow the leader!"

"Okay," Alex said. "Do it!"

Manny took a few steps on the field of snow. He looked back. Alex carefully put his feet exactly in Manny's tracks. Behind them the tracks looked like only one person had been there.

"Cool," Manny said. "See if you can keep up." He took giant steps in the snow. Alex followed perfectly. Manny swerved, his tracks forming a huge S on the field. Alex put his boots carefully where Manny had walked. Feet side by side, Manny kangaroo jumped through the snow. Alex jumped too, landing in the prints.

"This is like following Jesus," Alex said. "We travel in his footsteps, doing the types of things he did."

"Jesus sent the Holy Spirit to help us follow him," Manny said. "The Holy Spirit lives inside us and helps us all the way." Manny came to a frozen creek. He took gentle steps onto the snow-covered ice, Alex close behind him. With a cracking sound, the ice broke. Both boys sank into the cold water. Thankfully it wasn't deep.

"Except Jesus knows where he's going!" Alex said as the freezing water soaked his socks. "The Holy Spirit wouldn't lead us onto thin ice."

Your Turn

1. This week, how will following Jesus make a difference in your life?
2. What's a way you can show you are following Jesus?

Prayer

God, even though I can't see you, you guide my steps. Amen.

Being a Christian Means Following Jesus

Since we live by the Spirit, let us keep in step with the Spirit.
– Galatians 5:25

Careful Footsteps

There are things that can help you figure out how to follow Jesus without losing your way. From the list, pick out what you think will help you follow Jesus. In the footprints, write the ones that seem most important to you.

Bible	Christian	Worship	Love
Parents	Praying	Friends	Arguing
Cheating	Anger	Greed	Complaining

Prayer

God, I know that the best way I can please you is to follow Jesus. Thank you for the Holy Spirit, who lives in me and helps me. Amen.

Being a Christian Means Following Jesus

Since we live by the Spirit, let us keep in step with the Spirit.
– Galatians 5:25

Prayer Time

It's time for bed and time for prayers. Circle everything in the picture that might keep you from paying attention to God.

Prayer

God, I want to pray every day, but sometimes I get distracted. Please help me to remember to pray because I want to keep in step with you. Amen.

Being a Christian Means Following Jesus

Since we live by the Spirit, let us keep in step with the Spirit.
– Galatians 5:25

Listening to God

Chang raised his hand in Sunday school.

The teacher, Mrs. Carlyle, said, "Yes, Chang?"

"I've been reading my Bible," Chang said, "but sometimes I don't understand. Listen to this: 'Look to the Lord and his strength; seek his face always.' What does it mean to seek God's face?"

Mrs. Carlyle looked out her window, her back turned to Chang. "What do you think it means?"

"It sounds like one of those books with hidden pictures," Chang said. "God doesn't hide from us, does he?"

Mrs. Carlyle continued to stare out the window. "I don't think so. Any other ideas?"

Chang felt funny talking to his teacher's back. "Can't you tell me what it means?"

"First, let me ask you a question," Mrs. Carlyle said. "How do you think our conversation is going right now?"

"Not so good," Chang said. "I'm trying to talk to you, but you won't even look at me."

Mrs. Carlyle turned from the window. "When people pay attention to one another, they talk face-to-face, right?"

"So when the Bible says to seek God's face," Chang said, "it means pay attention to God. It's like facing people when they talk to you."

"Exactly right," Mrs. Carlyle said.

Your Turn

1. How do you pay attention to God?

_____

Prayer

God, I want us to be face-to-face friends. I won't turn my back on you, and I know you will never turn your back on me. Amen.

Being a Christian Means Following Jesus

Since we live by the Spirit, let us keep in step with the Spirit.
– Galatians 5:25

Producing Good Fruit

The Bible says you live by the Spirit. When you do, you will want to do the things that please God. Sometimes this is called this doing "good works." Good works come from God's Spirit just like fruit comes from a good tree. Ask an adult to help you think of more fruit that people can produce when they are trying to follow Jesus. Add those words to the apples on the tree. Which of these are you going to work on?

Prayer

God, I like getting smarter and better every day. I want to become more like you. Please keep working on me. Amen.

Being a Christian Means Following Jesus

Since we live by the Spirit, let us keep in step with the Spirit.
– Galatians 5:25

How Can I Help?

You can share God's love by helping people. The Holy Spirit will help you think of people who might be thankful if you helped them. Write their names on the lines below the picture.

Helping _____ with homework.

Helping _____ with yardwork.

Practice pitching and catching with _____.

Inviting _____ to go to church with me.

Prayer

God, one of the ways I can share your love is by helping people. That's what I want to do. Help me think of ways I can help people and share your love. Amen.

Being a Christian Means Following Jesus

Since we live by the Spirit, let us keep in step with the Spirit.
– Galatians 5:25

My Light

God wants you to be a light who shines for him. Change one letter in each word to get a good rule to live by.

PET   YOUN   GIGHT   FHINE

_____   _____   _____   _____

Prayer

God, use my eyes and ears and thoughts to light me up with your goodness. I pray that people will want to know why so I can tell them about you. Amen.

Make God Happy by Helping Others

Do not forget to do good and to share with others,
for with such sacrifices God is pleased.
– Hebrews 13:16

The Sucker

Trey and Ian were at the skateboard park near their school. As they strapped on their pads and tightened their helmet straps, Trey said, "Have you seen *Revenge of the Mutant Monster* yet?"

Ian had been waiting months for it to open at the theater. He loved monster movies. He even had an action figure based on *Mutant Monster*. The new movie was supposed to be better than the first one. "No," Ian said. "I might have to wait for a while."

"You had the money all saved up," Trey said. "What happened?" He rode his skateboard through a valley and up the opposite slope, reversed at the top, and came back toward Ian.

"I gave it away," Ian said. "A missionary came to our church and told us about his work in an orphanage in Africa."

"You gave your money to help an orphanage?" Trey said. "You're kidding me! That must have been a measly ten dollars."

"Every little bit helps," Ian said. "Sometimes the orphanage doesn't have food or medicine for the kids. I wanted to help."

"What a sucker!" Trey said. "You should have gone to the movie. Now you've got no money and no movie."

"But I know some orphans will have dinner tonight," Ian said.

Your Turn

1. Do you think Trey or Ian is right? Why do you think so?

_____

_____

Prayer

God, you have given so much to me. I want to share what I have with people who don't have as much. Give me a generous heart. Amen.

Make God Happy by Helping Others

Do not forget to do good and to share with others,
for with such sacrifices God is pleased.
– Hebrews 13:16

A Better Movie

Ian gave money to help children who have no parents to take care of them. Maybe his money will be used to buy food, or clothes, or schoolbooks. Use your imagination to think of what other kind of help Ian's money might buy. On the movie screen, draw a picture of the kids getting help from people who care about them.

Prayer

God, you gave me the gift of eternal life with you. I want to give gifts to people who need some help. Amen.

Make God Happy by Helping Others

Do not forget to do good and to share with others,
for with such sacrifices God is pleased.
– Hebrews 13:16

God's Sacrifice

Have you ever made a sacrifice for God? Have you ever given up something you cared about so you could please God? Even if you have never done that for God, God has done that for you. To learn about the sacrifice God made for you, fill in the missing letters. Hint: You will need four "O's," two "A's," two "E's," and one "I."

G_D G_V_
H_S _N_
_ND _NLY
S_N.

Prayer

God, thank you for your sacrifice for me. Even though Jesus is your only Son, you didn't hesitate to have him die in my stead on the cross. Because of that, I am able to spend eternity with you. I love you so much! Amen.

Make God Happy by Helping Others

Do not forget to do good and to share with others,
for with such sacrifices God is pleased.
– Hebrews 13:16

What Matters Most

Ian walked up the drive with his skateboard under his arm. His mother was in the yard pulling weeds from her flower garden. She wiped sweat from her face and said, "How is my favorite son?"

Ian was her only son, and he usually smiled at the joke. Not now though. "Trey said I'm a sucker," Ian said. "I told him I gave money to help an orphanage in Africa, and he said I threw away my money."

"Do you feel like you wasted your money?" his mother asked.

Ian sat on the ground next to his mom. "When I think of those kids in Africa, I am glad I could help."

"Yes," his mother said. "They have a hard time. Without help, I don't know what would happen to them."

"People matter more than movies. That's why I gave ten dollars," Ian said. "But I'm still sad I can't see the movie."

"That is called sacrifice," his mom said. "Giving up something you want to help someone else. God was pleased by your sacrifice."

"Mom, I'm glad I helped the orphanage," Ian said.

Your Turn

1. Write down what you would tell Ian about his sacrifice.
2. What have you given up for God?

_____

_____

_____

_____

Prayer

God, I don't mind giving up things sometimes to help others. Amen.

Make God Happy by Helping Others

Do not forget to do good and to share with others,
for with such sacrifices God is pleased.
– Hebrews 13:16

A Respect List

One of the ways you can do good to others is by respecting them. Make a list of people in your life that you want to show respect to. The words below will get you started. (If you have trouble reading the list, hold the book up to a mirror. That will help.)

Prayer

God, please show me how to be respectful even when I don't agree with others. I really need some help on this. Thanks. Amen.

Make God Happy by Helping Others

*Do not forget to do good and to share with others,
for with such sacrifices God is pleased.*
– Hebrews 13:16

Little Things Matter

God likes you to share with others. Even if all you can do seems small, you can still make things better for someone and please God. With God's help, small things can lead to big things.

Check out the little things below and draw a line connecting each one to the big thing it might lead to.

Prayer

Jesus, help me find big ways and small ways I can help people in your name. Amen.

Make God Happy by Helping Others

Do not forget to do good and to share with others,
for with such sacrifices God is pleased.
– Hebrews 13:16

Making a Difference

Did you know that even a small thing can be used by God? You might be surprised what a difference something small could mean in someone else's life. Look at the sets of pictures below and circle the differences.

Prayer

God, I am glad you can use my large and small sacrifices to help people. I am glad I can make a difference in someone's life. Amen.

Your Heart Reaches for God

You, God, are my God, earnestly I seek you; I thirst for you
– Psalm 63:1

Point North

Max loved to look at his grandfather's rock collection. The collection had crystals and stones from all over the world.

"What's this?" Max asked. He picked up a gray, lightweight stone.

"That is pumice," Grandpa said. "It comes from volcanoes. It's the only rock I know that will float on water."

"Cool!" Max said. "Is that gold?" He held a yellow, shiny piece of rock.

"That rock has iron in it," Grandpa said. "It's called fool's gold."

Max grinned. "It fooled me." Then he noticed a gray stone shaped like a pencil. It was about two inches long. A string was tied around the middle. "Why is that rock tied with a string?"

Grandpa lifted the rock by the string. "Lodestone," Grandpa said. "It's magnetic like a compass. Held by a string, it always points true north."

Max pushed the rock. As soon as he stopped, the stone swung back to the same place. He moved it again, but it swung back to pointing north.

"God made us that way too," Grandpa said. "Our hearts are always reaching for God. We will never be truly happy if we turn away from God."

Your Turn

1. Are people who know God happier than people who don't? Explain.

_____

_____

_____

_____

Prayer

God, I can't imagine trying to live without you. You are my super best friend. I will always want more and more of you. Amen.

Your Heart Reaches for God

You, God, are my God, earnestly I seek you; I thirst for you
– Psalm 63:1

Get Smart

If you can figure out the secret code on this treasure map, you'll know about something more valuable than rubies and diamonds. In the code, first scratch out every X. Then scratch out every M. Finally, scratch out every Z. Don't miss any! Are you wise enough to read the message in the letters that are left? Write it at the bottom of the page.

Prayer

Lord, I know the only way I can get truly wise is to get to know you better. To do that, I need to read my Bible and pray. I know you will help me get wisdom. Thank you. Amen.

Your Heart Reaches for God

You, God, are my God, earnestly I seek you; I thirst for you
– Psalm 63:1

Which Way?

There are many good things in life, but there can be only one thing that is most important of all. Look at the things circling the compass. Many of them are worth having. Draw the compass hand to the one that is most important in your life.

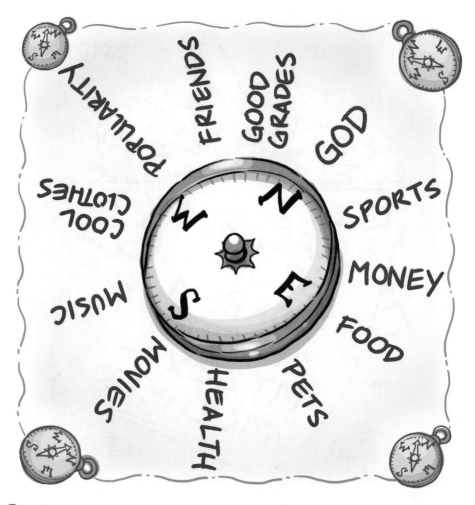

Prayer

God, I know that the right way for me is to go where you lead me. Your Word is like food and drink to me. I need it to live. Thank you. Amen.

your Heart Reaches for God

You, God, are my God, earnestly I seek you; I thirst for you
– Psalm 63:1

The Reminder Rock

Max loved looking at Grandpa's rock collection. "You have so many. Do you have a favorite?"

Grandpa pulled a case from the shelf. "I wasn't much older than you when I found this one. I don't know if it's my favorite, but I was sure excited when I saw it lying in my pan." He took out a pea-sized rock and dropped it into Max's palm. The lumpy stone was gray and red.

"In your pan?" Max asked "Were you cooking?"

"No," Grandpa said. "Sometimes rock collectors use pans and water to sift stones from dirt along a river. That's how I found this ruby."

"This is a real ruby?" Max asked. "Is it worth a million dollars?"

Grandpa laughed. "No, it is small and rough and only worth a few dollars. But I know something even better than rubies."

"Diamonds?" Max asked.

Grandpa shook his head. "Wisdom. Wisdom means living the way God teaches. That will make a person happier than having a pocketful of rubies. Keep that one, Max."

"Wow, thanks!" Max said.

"Carry it in your pocket to remind you that serving God is the most precious thing of all," Grandpa said.

your Turn

1. Why does the Bible say wisdom is so precious?

_____

_____

_____

Prayer

I want to be wise, God—wise enough to follow Jesus all the way. He is a lot better than rubies and diamonds. Amen.

Your Heart Reaches for God

You, God, are my God, earnestly I seek you; I thirst for you
– Psalm 63:1

Praying Is Easy

You can probably think of lots of things to talk to God about. You can tell God about your day. You can ask for help with problems. You can tell God you are sorry for bad things you did. You can ask God to bless people you love. If you ever run out of things to talk about with God, here is a prayer you can use. The prayer is in a secret code.

To break the code, move each letter forward one place in the alphabet. For example, if you see an A, change it to B, the next letter in the alphabet. If you find an N, change it into O. Get it? Can you figure out this prayer?

Prayer

God, I am so glad you want to talk to me. If you have time for me, I sure have time for you! Amen.

Your Heart Reaches for God

You, God, are my God, earnestly I seek you; I thirst for you
– Psalm 63:1

God's Word Satisfies

When you spend time with God, it's like finding a pool of fresh water on a hot day. Your thirst will be satisfied when you drink. Help the boy navigate through the maze to find the pool of fresh water. You can use a crayon, a marker, or trace the route with your finger.

Prayer

God, I want to grow closer to you. Encourage me to read my Bible and pray every day. Amen.

Your Heart Reaches for God

You, God, are my God, earnestly I seek you; I thirst for you
– Psalm 63:1

Jesus Is the Key

Have you asked Jesus to lead you and to forgive your sins? If you have, that means your name is written in heaven. Write your name in the cloud as a reminder that Jesus loves you. Copy the page and post it on your bedroom wall.

Prayer

God, I have learned so much about you. I don't want to stop now! I know that even if I live to be super old, I'll never know everything there is to know about you. Thank you for forgiving me and for making me your child. I love you! Amen.

Answer Key

Page 10

Page 11

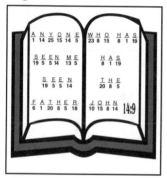

ANYONE WHO HAS
1 14 25 15 14 5   23 8 15   8 1 19

SEEN ME   HAS
19 5 5 14 13 5   8 1 19

SEEN   THE
19 5 5 14   20 8 5

FATHER.   JOHN
6 1 20 8 5 18   10 15 8 14   14:9

Page 38

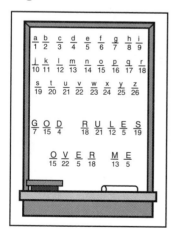

a b c d e f g h i
1 2 3 4 5 6 7 8 9

j k l m n o p q r
10 11 12 13 14 15 16 17 18

s t u v w x y z
19 20 21 22 23 24 25 26

G O D   R U L E S
7 15 4   18 21 12 5 19

O V E R   M E
15 22 5 18   13 5

Page 55

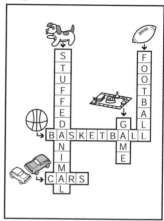

Page 56

a b c d e f g h i
1 2 3 4 5 6 7 8 9

j k l m n o p q r
10 11 12 13 14 15 16 17 18

s t u v w x y z
19 20 21 22 23 24 25 26

p u t
16 21 20

g o d
7 15 4

f i r s t
6 9 18 19 20

Page 60

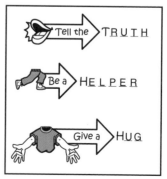

374

Page 63

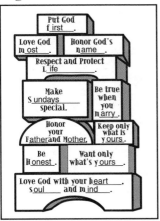

Page 66

Those who believe
in His Name,
He gave the
right to
become
children
of God.
John 1:12

Page 70

I WILL NOT
1 2 3 4 5 6 7 8

FORGET YOU!
9 10 11 12 13 14 15 16 17

Page 73

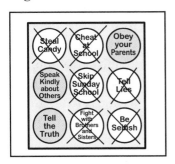

Page 74

Page 101

Page 102

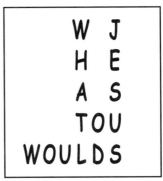

Page 104

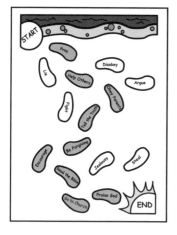

Page 167

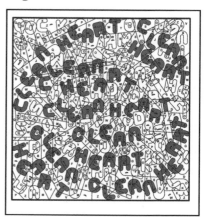

Page 130

Page 168

Page 141

MERCY
9 2 11 10 13

Page 158

JESUS
2 4 5 8 5

Page 174

Thank You, God, for sending <u>Jesus</u> to die on the <u>cross</u> for me. I know my <u>sins</u> are <u>forgiven</u>. I want to <u>obey</u> Your <u>Word</u> and <u>serve</u> You. Thank You for <u>loving me</u>. Thank You for <u>forgiving me</u>. Thank You that some day I can live with You in <u>heaven</u>.

Page 175

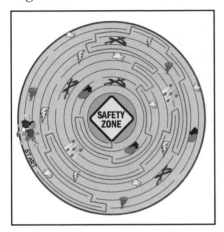

Page 183

U E S J S
J E S U S

Page 196

For my thoughts are not your thoughts.

Page 202

Page 207

Harsh — Kind
Hateful — Soft
Mean — Gentle
Gruff — Happy
Hard — Loving
Angry — Calm

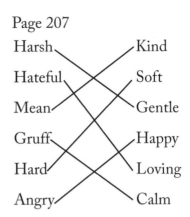

Page 207

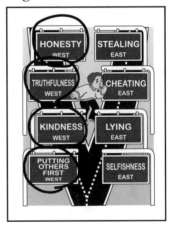

Page 213

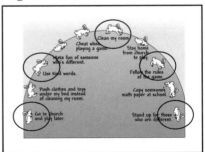

Page 217

Page 221
God is with me wherever I go so I
will not be afraid.

Page 225

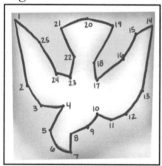

Page 228

Page 228

Page 232

Page 234

Page 235

Page 238

Page 239

Page 241

Page 241

Page 246

Page 246

FIALMF TLWHE GWOLOFD WSHLEP-FHWELRFWD
(I AM THE GOOD SHEPHERD)

Page 251

The ground of a certain rich man produced a good crop. He thought to himself, "What shall I do? I have no place to store my crops." Then he said, "This is what I'll do. I will tear down my barns and build bigger ones, and there I will store all my grain and my goods. And I'll say to myself, 'You have plenty of good things laid up for many years. Take life easy; eat, drink and be merry.'" But God said to him, "You fool! This very night your life will be demanded from you. Then who will get what you have prepared for yourself?"

Page 253

Page 255

ULITREV FH ULI
FORGIVE US FOR
WLRMT DILMT
DOING WRONG
ZH DV ULITREV
AS WE FORGIVE
LGSVIH
OTHERS

Page 262

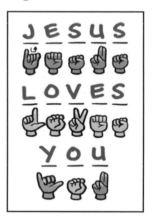

JESUS LOVES YOU

Page 269

Change the 1's to E's; the 2's to I's; the 3's to O's; and the 4's to U's

2'm g32ng t3 f3ll3w J1s4s
I'm going to follow Jesus

Page 279

Page 281

Page 293

Page 302

Page 304

Do not worship any god except me.

Do not make idols.

Do not misuse my name.

Remember that the Sabbath Day belongs to me. No one is to work on that day.

Respect your father and your mother.

Do not murder.

Be faithful in marriage.

Do not steal.

Do not tell lies about others.

Do not want anything that belongs to someone else.

Page 302

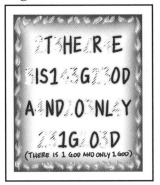

Page 314

Page 333

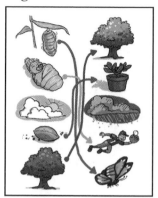

Page 319

Page 322

Our Father in heaven, hallowed be your name. Your kingdom come, your will be done, on earth as it is in heaven. Give us today our daily bread. And forgive us our debts, as we also have forgiven our debtors. And lead us not into temptation, but deliver us from the evil one. Amen.

Page 336

Page 337

Jesus Christ is the same yesterday and today and forever.

Page 343

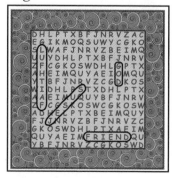

Page 349

Page 351

Page 354

Page 358
Let Your Light Shine

Page 361

Page 363

Page 364

Page 365

Page 370

Page 371

ROSEKIDZ IS PROUD TO PRESENT

Certificate of Completion

for Gotta Have God One-Year Devotional for Boys 6-9

to _____ on _____
(name) (date)

Congratulations!

May God bless you in every way
as you continue to grow in the
knowledge, grace, and love of our Jesus Christ.

Ages 6-9   Ages 10-12

L46971   L46972

Gotta Have God!
52 Week Devotional for Boys
380-388 pages, Softcover, Full Color Illustrations.

Gotta Have God!
232-248 pages, Softcover, Full Color Illustrations.
Jesus knows all about being a boy because he was one! Gotta Have God helps young men learn how much he loves them and wants to be the model for their lives. Each age-based book, for boys ages 2–5, ages 6–9, and ages 10–12, includes devotions and activities designed to help boys understand how they can grow to be strong Christian men. Over 100 devotionals in each book.

L46961   L46962   L46963

L46964   L46965   L46966

L46967   L46968   L46969

Find more great stuff by visiting our website: www.hendricksonrose.com

Time Crashers

Ages 8-12, 200 pages, Paperback, Illustrated.

A time machine, three friends, and a dad who is lost in the past. That's the Time Crashers Series. Loaded with humor, adventure, and mind-bending puzzles to solve, our heroes find themselves transported to another time and place and meet real characters from the past. With danger (or shenanigans!) at the turn of every page, the fate of the Time Crashers is in your hands with this interactive choose-your-own-adventure book! Each book in the series sends the reader on an action-packed journey where they learn to trust God for all their choices. In this epic choose-your-own-adventure, you get to decide the fate of Ethan, Jake, and Spencer! Ages 8–12.

Choose Your Own Ending inside History!

L48702

L48701

L48703

L48704

Bill the Warthog Mysteries

Ages 7–12 years, 112 pages, Paperback, Illustrated.

I don't suppose you have a friend who is a warthog. You probably
don't have a friend who is a professional detective, either. So it's
very unlikely that you have a friend who's both. But I do."So begins
the adventures of Nick Sayga and his friend Bill, a warthog detective,
in Full Metal Trench Coat, the first book in the new Bill the Warthog
Mysteries series. As Bill fights kid's "crimes," such as investigating
celebrity soccer shoes and broken skateboard helmets, he also teaches
Nick and his friends about the Armour of God. Kids will love trying
to figure out each chapter's mystery as they enjoy the zany antics of
Bill, Nick and their friends. And they will laugh at Bill's crazy attempts to
fit in with kids, even putting tennis balls on his tusks so he can join the soccer
team without risk of injuring the palyers! Bill the Warthog Mysteries: Full Metal
Trench Coat will bring laughter and learning to preteens, and kids of all ages!

L48301	L48302	L48303
L48304	L48305	L48306
L48307	L48308	L48309

Find more great stuff by visiting our website: www.hendricksonrose.com